"*University Matters* is thorough, well-presented and loaded with factual tips. There's lots of good information on preparing for exams, communicating with professors and really useful checklists. I would recommend that anyone planning on attending university for the first time pick up a copy of this book and have it handy as an ongoing reference guide."

Sharon Bros, parent of a September '05 university-bound student

"This book is an informative and interactive tool for students as they prepare for university or college. It provides a great deal of insight into the challenges, and exciting new experiences, that students face daily, and offers new ideas and strategies for excelling."

Lindsay Mossman, Vice President Student Issues,
Carleton Student Union Association

"I think *University Matters* will be very useful for graduating high school students. Many high school students have a fear of university and this book should help them conquer that fear."

Tomo Dadic, University of Guelph,
Business Administration '07

"This is the most important book you will read during your university career."
Paul Mitchell, recent MBA graduate

"Wow, what a lot of useful info. I found once I started reading, I couldn't stop."
Christine Tordon, Director of University Admissions, Ashbury College.

"*University Matters* is the first resource I have seen that has so much information at a glance. This is a must read for every graduating student interested in university or college. Parents will find this a valuable resource as well. The suggestions on dealing with classes and professors' expectations are very valuable, and your points to students who feel they have selected the wrong program are supportive and important and will help in the areas of retention and success. I will definitely recommend *University Matters* to my students and see it as a great resource to use within the guidance curriculum."

Patty Seravalle, Head of Guidance and Career Education,
Heart Lake Secondary School, Peel Board of Education

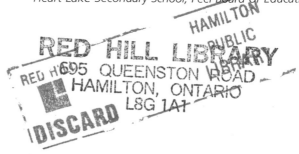

UNIVERSITY MATTERS

PREPARE FOR THE CHALLENGES • REALIZE YOUR POTENTIAL

Sharron McIntyre, MBA
Michael McIntyre, PhD, CA

With Alison Trant, MD, CCFP
Illustrated by Eric Chan

Published by Creative Bound International Inc.
on behalf of University Matters

ISBN 1-894439-20-1
Printed and bound in Canada

The author and publisher have made every attempt to locate and acknowledge copyright holders of quoted material. If we have inadvertently made any errors or omissions, kindly inform us so that we may correct any future reprints and editions. Thank you.

Production by Creative Bound International Inc.
    Gail Baird, Managing Editor
    Wendelina O'Keefe, Creative Director
    1-800-287-8610   www.creativebound.com
Illustrations by Eric Chan   http://ericchan.ca

Library and Archives Canada Cataloguing in Publication

McIntyre, Sharron
        University matters : prepare for the challenges & realize your potential / Sharron McIntyre, Michael McIntyre ; with contributions by Alison Trant ; illustrated by Eric Chan.

Includes bibliographical references.
ISBN 1-894439-20-1

        1. College student orientation--Canada--Handbooks, manuals, etc.
2. College students--Canada--Life skills guides. 3. Study skills--
Handbooks, manuals, etc. I. McIntyre, Michael   II. Trant, Alison
III. Title.

LB2343.34.C3M32 2005   378.1'98'0971   C2005-903432-7

For our children

Erin, Paul, Andrew and Tori

Alec, Matt and Maggie

Acknowledgements

This book would not be the incredible resource that it is without the input of many people. Thank you to the students, professors, graduates, parents and guidance counsellors who have generously shared their thoughts, opinions, insights and experiences with us, and by extension, with you, our readers of *University Matters*. Their concern for your welfare, and their sincere desire to see you succeed is heart-warming indeed.

In particular, we would like to thank Joanne Lalonde-Hayes who led by example, founding the hugely popular More Time Moms, www.moretimemoms.com. Joanne's encouragement, support and "you can do it" attitude have been invaluable. Her energy has infused our text, and even if only a little bit rubs off on our readers, we will all be better off for it.

Thanks also to our friends, and unconditional supporters, Trish Dusting, Christine Jackson and Dee Patterson. This book benefits from their generosity of spirit, their wise "advice and counsel," and their sharp-pencilled, hard-nosed editing!

A special thanks to Wendy O'Keefe and Gail Baird and their team at Creative Bound International Inc., who were responsible for the design, pre-press work and production of the book.

And last but not least, many thanks to the extended McIntyre family, in particular Jim, Joe, Maureen, Karen Moore, Erin, Nora Kirkpatrick, Paul and Jennifer.

Contents

About the Authors

The authors of *University Matters* have collectively either attended or taught at eight different Canadian universities. So to some extent, this is a "been there—done that" story. Having said this, the authors' respective experiences at university have varied widely. Two of them learned how to enjoy life and succeed in university by doing much of what you will read in this book. The other learned a lot of the same things by neglecting to do them. We are not sure which is the "road less travelled" among university students, but all the authors agree that you will enjoy all aspects of university life much more if you use *University Matters*. University students surround Sharron and Mike. Their daughter recently graduated from the University of Toronto and one son and four nieces are currently studying at McGill, University of New Brunswick and Carleton. Despite the authors' different university lifestyles, they all agree that the university years are a terrific adventure full of personal, social and intellectual growth. They hope and wish that when you walk up to receive your degree a few years from now, you will feel the same way.

Sharron McIntyre

Sharron was born and raised in the UK and commenced her post-secondary education at John Abbott College in Montreal shortly after her family moved to Canada. From there, she moved on to Concordia University, Loyola Campus, to take a Bachelor of Commerce. She was a straight-A student graduating with distinction and with the marketing medal. She completed an MBA at the University of Toronto while working on Bay Street in the financial sector. A number of years later, while Mike worked on his Ph.D. at Queen's University, Sharron spent her time teaching in the undergraduate business program and helped students with career planning. The students' enthusiasm, energy and passion were an inspiring and refreshing change for Sharron. She is the mother of four children and after many years as a corporate finance professional now spends her time devising ways to help university students.

Michael McIntyre

Mike obtained a Bachelor of Commerce degree from Queen's University and earned a CA while working for Coopers & Lybrand in Toronto. He completed an MBA at York University while working as a public accountant, and after sixteen years in the work force, returned to Queen's where he earned a Ph.D. in management, specializing in derivative securities and risk management. During his first couple of years as an undergraduate, Mike divided his time among bridge, squash, socializing and academics. Although this book encourages diversity of interests, Mike didn't get the percentage allocations of his time quite right until his later years in the undergraduate program. This book benefits both from Mike's conversion from the "dark side of unbalanced priorities" and from observations as a faculty member. Mike is a faculty member at the Eric Sprott School of Business, Carleton University and, from time to time, a visiting fellow at Queen's University's International Study Centre at Herstmonceux Castle, UK. He has also taught at the University of Toronto and Queen's University. Mike has become a proponent of hard work balanced with play thanks to a number of factors, not least of which are the repeated "encouragements" of his wife Sharron. Today, in addition to being an academic and running his own risk management consulting business, Mike spends his time helping his son and other students adopt the philosophies set out in this book, and revels in each student's successes.

Alison Trant

Alison completed degrees in Biology and Medicine at the University of Ottawa, and graduated Magna Cum Laude. She is currently practicing family medicine in the Ottawa area and is the mother of three children. Alison achieved her goals through hard work and organization. To successfully juggle life as a physician, wife, mother and exercise enthusiast, Alison must continue to carefully anticipate and schedule her many diverse commitments. She is confident the skills students learn in this book will be very useful—not just in university, but in later life as well. Alison's interest in the prevention of sexually transmitted infections stems from her medical work in family practice and her role as a parent of soon-to-be teenagers. The information found in Appendix 4 about sexual infections will help students become well-informed and make wise choices to prevent illness.

The parts of this book that stress studying hard, being prepared and completing work on time (or even better, ahead of schedule) arise primarily out of the university life experiences of Sharron and Alison. It certainly worked for them with one being an award-winning student, and the other excelling in undergraduate studies to the point of gaining acceptance in medical school. Although Sharron enjoyed being a successful undergraduate student, she now wishes she had not been so single-minded in her pursuit of academics. She pressured herself to excel academically because she was the first person in her entire extended family to attend university. In hindsight, she realizes that life could have been richer sooner had she devoted a little less time to academics and a little more time to the broader set of experiences university offers. She does admit to attending her fair share of beer bashes, but only if her papers were up to standard! The parts of this book that argue for balance and enjoyment of all that university offers arise out of what Sharron feels she could have experienced during her undergraduate years. Alison is constantly striving to achieve balance as her life progresses. Having spent too much time on academics while at school, and to this day often too much time at work to relax, she has yet to find it.

• • •

About the Illustrator: Eric Chan

One of the great pleasures of writing this book has been the privilege of working with the talented young artist Eric Chan. Eric commenced his post-secondary education at Algonquin College, completing a program in Computer Engineering Technology–Computing Science with Honours. He is currently a student in the Bachelor of Information Technology–Interactive Multimedia and Design program at Carleton University. In addition to working hard on his studies, Eric spends time developing Web sites, and illustrating. His most recent success was his nomination for "Best Canadian Student" for his on-line Flash portfolio at the FITC Design Competition in Toronto in April 2005.

Preface

Canada has the highest rate of post-secondary schooling in the world with 71 percent of youth going to college or university by their early twenties. Students attending university represent 33 percent of Canadian youth, and enrolment is continuing to increase.[1] Each spring there are over 100,000 students who have been accepted at a Canadian university and are planning to attend in September. We call these students "First Years." This book is for them.

While *University Matters* speaks directly to First Years, it is also a valuable resource for parents of First Years. The issues we address will help parents understand what their young adult children are going through. When graduates talk to First Years, their message is often a trite "These are the best years of your life." We forget all too easily the stresses we faced at the same stage in our lives. Reading through the chapter indices will remind parents of the many demands on their children. *University Matters* is a complete and concise source of information for parents to use as a basis for supporting their children as they go through university, and to use as a guide for evaluating a son's or daughter's approach to university life.

During their final year of high school, students spend a lot of time investigating career choices and universities. Making the right choice of university involves matching an individual student's desires to what a university has to offer in a number of important areas, such as the field of study, extracurricular activities, technological capabilities, size of the surrounding community, class size, and student-to-teacher ratios. Many students obtain advice from high school guidance counsellors to help them choose the university and program that are right for them. Some students tour university campuses and meet with university liaison staff to help them with their decisions. When the acceptance comes, the hard work is really just beginning. It is time to get ready to go to university, and the time to start is now!

There is a lot to do in the months between acceptance and attendance, so First Years need to start using *University Matters* as soon as high school ends. There is a big period of adjustment for First Years during the important first few weeks of university.

---

1 *Who pursues postsecondary education, who leaves and why: Results from the Youth in Transition Survey.* Statistics Canada, Catalogue no. 81-595-MIE – No. 026.

This book sets out what they need to do and what they need to know to make the best choices in this critical and often confusing period. For most First Years, the social and academic environment in university is much different from the high school environment. *University Matters* presents helpful material on time management, academic skills and life skills that will help students successfully make this challenging transition. This book is unique because it addresses all aspects of the life challenges First Years face. *University Matters* is a coalescence of insights and advice from an actively teaching university professor, students at all stages of university, and graduates from various years, disciplines and universities. *University Matters* provides First Years with an opportunity to learn from the successes, observations, and yes, even the errors, of a broad range of individuals who are living or have lived the First Year experience.

University Matters' overriding goal is to provide information to First Years that will make their university experience as fulfilling as possible. As you can see from the description of our backgrounds, some of us have erred on the side of excessive devotion to studying, which in some ways diminished our overall university experience, while one of us spent far too much time on sports and social life. While singularity of purpose can achieve a lot, we are not sure it qualifies as making university a fulfilling experience in its broadest sense. Our underlying philosophy is that First Years are more likely to make good choices if they are well informed about the whole university experience. So *University Matters* is filled with descriptions of circumstances that typically challenge First Years, and suggests strategies for coping with them. We believe that being well-equipped will enable First Years to live rich and fulfilling lives while achieving their academic goals.

Section One of *University Matters* is entitled Getting Ready. In this section we present a long list of tasks for First Years to address, whether they plan to live at home or live away. First Years need to get physically and emotionally ready for the challenges they are about to experience. There is a lot to do, so they need to start preparing in July and August. The goal of *University Matters* is to help them get as much done as they can so they aren't burdened during the first few weeks of term when time is very short and anxiety can be high. First Years should read this section well before commencing their first term at university.

Section Two is entitled Staying Organized. In this section we present ideas that will help First Years manage their time effectively. Time management is a crucial life skill. It is all the more so at university where time can be a deceitful partner, tricking you into thinking it is moving more slowly than it is. First Years need to know how to manage their personal and academic commitments by the beginning of the first week of classes. This section should be read in July or August, and then revisited as the term starts.

Section Three is entitled Academic Skills, and **Section Four** is entitled Life Skills. In these sections we address a broad range of topics intended to help First Years get the most out of both their academic and social lives at university. Indeed, part of the message in these sections is that the interaction of intelligent academic decisions and intelligent social decisions enhances all aspects of one's university experience. Although we recommend that First Years read these sections before commencing university, some may prefer to read some sections in July and August while leaving others until the need to refer to them arises. First Years who prefer the latter approach should familiarize themselves with the content of these sections to ensure they make good choices about what to read and what to defer. For example, Section Three, which addresses effective note taking, a skill most students will need right from the start, shouldn't be left until later.

The appendices include useful information for First Years. Appendix 4 is particularly important. Here, using straight-forward language that is medically accurate, Dr. Trant addresses the sexually transmitted infections ("STIs") that First Years could encounter. This is vital information that all young adults need to know because there are serious health risks that come with sexual activity.

University Matters is intended to be used with a day planner, preferably the University Matters Student Planner, available from www.universitymatters.ca, which has been specifically designed to help students manage their busy life.

To each First Year who reads this book,
we wish you every success. And just as importantly,
we wish you enjoyment and fulfillment during university life.

To each parent, we wish you much patience and
pleasure as you watch your child's entry into adulthood.

Getting Ready

SECTION ONE

• • •

Getting Ready

It is easy to think of your departure for university as a matter of packing up as much stuff as you think you'll need, and taking off. Or, if you plan on living at home, you might see it as a simple matter of heading off to classes on the first day, but this time to university instead of high school. The reality is that university life is a major shift from what you are used to. A small investment in some "thinking" and "doing" ahead of time will significantly improve the experience for you. This section is designed to help you prepare to make the most of your new life at university.

Biggest Challenges
- Believing you can do it
- Taking the time to handle administrative matters during the summer
- Settling in and adjusting to your new environment

1. Getting Psyched

Life at university will be different from what you are used to, mainly because you will be so much more on your own than ever before. Even if you intend to live at home, you will be facing new decisions with less input from parents and others. Part of this phenomenon is that you are more grown-up than during your high school years, and many parents respond to this by consciously reducing their role in your life. The quantity and complexity of things that will be going on in your life and their inter-connections will force you to be the key decision-maker on how to run your life throughout university.

1.1   The road ahead

Most students have nagging worries as they get ready
to go to university:

- Will it be difficult to make new friends?
  - » It is easier than you think because everyone
    is in the same position. Keep a smile on your
    face and refer to Chapter 12.1 for helpful tips.
- Will the complexity and volume of workload be
  manageable?
  - » You will probably find the transition rather smooth and refreshing, in part
    because assignments at university can be more open-ended than you are
    used to, which allows you to explore your thoughts and develop new
    opinions. More time is devoted to "thinking" and "asking why" rather
    than to just "doing";
  - » The reading load can be quite heavy, but if you keep up as the term
    unfolds it will be manageable.
- Am I "smart" enough to complete university?
  - » You don't have to be "bright" to be successful, but you do have to study
    consistently, and make your academic studies a top priority;
  - » High school grades may not be good predictors of academic success at
    university. Interpersonal skills, adaptability and stress management are just
    as important, if not more so. These are discussed in Section Four.
- If I move away from home, how badly will I miss my best friends and family?
  - » You will make new friends quickly at university. You can maintain your
    close relationships via regular e-mail and solidify them during the holidays;
  - » The people around you will be facing the same concerns and challenges
    that you are facing, and this will help you knit together a new support
    structure early in the term.

Before your first term starts, take time to reflect upon the many new challenges
ahead of you. Start thinking about how you will handle them.

- Dealing with the impersonal university environment, especially on larger
  campuses:
  - » Large organizations can come across as impersonal. Try to see this as the
    university using very limited resources to cope with a large number of

---

2   c. f. Who pursues postsecondary education, who leaves and why: Results from the Youth in Transition
Survey. Statistics Canada, Catalogue no. 81-595-MIE – No. 026.

students. The administrators you meet probably have demanding jobs for this very reason. Look upon your interactions with them as an opportunity to brighten their day rather than as an opportunity to find fault;

> **Thirty-five** percent of university students feel like they are a number most or all of the time. [4]

» Remain patient when seeking help. University administration is concerned with the many pressures facing students. Behind the scenes every effort is being made to help students integrate into the community.[3]

- Managing your time and creating a daily structure to meet academic deadlines:
  » You will need to plan and use your time wisely if you wish to participate in the many activities that exist on campus in addition to working on your academic studies and possibly holding down a part-time job. Chapter 5 will help you become proficient at managing your varied obligations.
- Managing a financial budget:
  » Whether or not you personally pay for all or part of your university tuition and living expenses, you will be well aware of the significant financial cost of each year you attend university. This can add significant stress to your life;
  » You might be surprised at how quickly your money disappears. Some students have been known to spend their entire year's budget in the first term;
  » Use our Budgeting Spreadsheet, available at www.universitymatters.ca, to allocate your funds over the academic year. Make a plan and monitor your expenses. More details in Chapter 15.
- Making it a priority to spend time on exercise, eating healthy meals and getting enough sleep:
  » You need to nurture your mind, body and soul to have the energy to fully participate in campus life. Refer to Chapter 13;
  » In order to achieve this you need a comfortable living space where you feel "at home." More details in Chapter 14.
- Keeping marks in perspective:
  » Intellectual stimulation, reasoning and learning are just as important as marks. Sometimes they go hand in hand, but not always. Refer to Chapter 6.6.

---

3   See for example, Tam, P., "Carleton aims to keep students happier", *The Ottawa Citizen*, January 19, 2005, page C1.

4   c. f. Who pursues postsecondary education, who leaves and why: Results from the Youth in Transition Survey. Statistics Canada, Catalogue no. 81-595-MIE – No. 026.

64% Sixty-four percent of students rated their university as good or excellent in helping them develop effective study and learning skills.

56% Fifty-six percent of students rated their university as good or excellent in helping them develop skills to think logically and analytically.

52% Fifty-two percent of students rated their university as good or excellent in helping them develop skills for planning and completing projects.

52% Fifty-two percent of students rated their university as good or excellent in helping them develop skills to understand abstract reasoning.

50% Fifty percent of students rated their university as good or excellent in helping them develop skills to identify and solve problems.[5]

- A part-time job can put downward pressure on final marks:
  - » While this can be true, the story isn't completely negative. Some employers implicitly make an upward adjustment to take account of all the demands on a student, while others give credit for work experience that may more than compensate for the lower marks.
- Learning to cope with stress and problems and asking for help:
  - » Although there is a lot of emphasis on independence as you move from a home-oriented high school experience to a "you-oriented" university experience, this emphasis is misguided. Very few of us are independent, and many who are find life very lonely. Most of us look to our friends, colleagues, fellow students, roommates, academic advisors and others for support.

1.2   Believe in yourself

You are now "standing on your own two feet," developing your own expectations for your life at university. In order to be successful you will have to actively manage your commitments and precious time to meet your goals. While there is lots of help available, no one is likely to hand it to you.

- During high school, you may have depended on the encouragement of your mother, father or friends:
  - » Now, you need to look within yourself for the motivation to get something done.

---

5   Survey of Undergraduate University Students: University of Winnipeg, 2002, downloaded from http://www.uwinnipeg.ca/index/cms-filesystem-action?file=pdfs/future/cusc.pdf on April 6, 2005.

- Initially, you will appear to have more free time since you will be spending less time in class:
  - » Now, you are expected to spend more time studying on your own.
- One of the joys of living away from home is that no one will bother you about when to get up, when to go to class, when to eat, when to study or when to sleep. This is great because it won't be very often that someone will nag you to do something. But, on the other hand, you are left to your own devices:
  - » Now, you will need to "bother" yourself!
- Even if you are living at home, chances are your parents will play a much smaller role in your day-to-day life than they did during high school:
  - » Now, you will be left to manage the myriad of commitments in your life.

Self-reliance is what we should strive for. We can rely on ourselves to seek help from the people and resources around us to navigate life's challenges. We have to develop our ability to use what we have: our intelligence, our common sense, our creativity, our friends and associates to get where we want to go. We are not islands unto ourselves and there is no glory in trying to be so. We need our community to support us, and we should be prepared to lend a helping hand to others. "What goes around comes around."

The better you understand your personal goals, the more motivated you will be to work hard to achieve them. If you haven't contemplated this kind of thing before you may not have a clear idea of what is most important to you. To help focus your thinking, consider the following questions:

- What are your priorities, now and in the longer term?
- What do you want to get out of this experience?
- What skills do you want to develop?
- What new interests do you want to develop?
- What do you expect from your friends?
- What contributions do you want to make to your life and the lives of others?

When students arrive on campus, many are taken aback by things they hadn't anticipated. These are the most commonly cited:

- Feeling overwhelmed by the large number of students in introductory classes;
- How easy it is to fall behind in scheduled reading;
- How easy it is to gain weight;
- How different a roommate's habits and preferences can be;
- The huge number of on-campus opportunities other than studying;
- How quickly time flies, both through the day and through the term;
- How hard it is to say no to social opportunities despite looming academic deadlines.

- What do you really value?
- If people who know you well were to describe you or your qualities, what would you like them to honestly say about you?
- Are your extracurricular activities and volunteer work in-line with your personal goals?

Defining your goals and writing them down will help you become more successful. Be as specific as possible and be realistic with what you can achieve. You can always set higher goals once you have achieved your initial goals. It is much easier to make and implement a plan to achieve your goals if they are written down and if you reflect upon them regularly.

Record your aspirations on the Personal Goals Worksheet in your *University Matters Student Planner.*

- You will have many opportunities to reconsider the above questions as decisions are presented to you. Use those opportunities to reflect upon areas of your life that you'd like to improve upon and think about how you will do so.
- Assess your strengths and weaknesses, seeking input from close friends and family. Be confident in your abilities and have a positive attitude towards working on your weaknesses, both of which will lead to personal success.
- Many people are "successful" in this world, whether it is in their career or other life achievements, without having done well at school, let alone having a university degree. Your inner drive to achieve is just as important, if not more important, than a degree in hand. Only you can define your success.
- Someone, at some point, may have told you that you were a "failure." Don't let the opinions of others define your ambitions. It is a risky business to allow others to determine your self-worth:

» You are responsible for defining what success is for you, and then going out and achieving it on your terms;

» Set your own standards, and decide for yourself whether or not you have met them. When you have, congratulate yourself;

» When you don't meet those standards, ask yourself what went wrong and what can be improved for the next time, then forgive yourself and renew your resolve to do better;

» When someone disapproves even though you are meeting your own goals, or congratulates you when you aren't, look to what is important to you, and whether or not you have been faithful to your own personal standards.

Be prepared to make mistakes and to learn from them.

- Don't let a "failure" get you down. Use it as an opportunity to improve going forward. It is an indicator that you have to prepare more, or to move in a different direction.

- You might think failure to achieve a goal represents an erosion of your value as an individual, of your self-worth. Try to avoid this trap. If you never take a chance you will never fail, and who wants to go through life without ever taking a chance? Failure is part of exploring the world and trying new things.

> **"I have not failed,**
> I've just found 10,000 ways that won't work."
> Thomas A. Edison

1.3   Strive for balance

Success as a university student is about a lot more than good marks.

- University is a time to experiment and broaden your horizons. Try new sports, take interesting courses in disciplines that are new to you, and make new friends, all of which will help you grow and mature as an individual.

- Too much focus on one element of your university life to the exclusion of the others is going to lead to problems. For example, too much focus on academics might leave you isolated and lonely, but too much focus on socializing will compromise your

> **Balance** is the key to success. There is no question that learning at university is important, but although you are there to learn, you are also living your life. It is a journey that should be enjoyed, so balance work and fun.

studies and might leave you in fear of failing. If you are headed to a reputed "party school," have a firm deal with yourself about how much time you will socialize versus study:

» Aim to learn as much as you can by developing good study habits and make your academic workload your first priority. More details in Chapter 7;

» Many lifelong friendships are made at university. Pick friends that share your values.

The importance of different elements of your life—socializing, athletics and academics—will change depending on you and the circumstances you face. Think about which elements of your life deserve the most attention, and allocate your time and efforts accordingly. With experience this will come naturally to you.

University is full of wonderful people, points of view from all ends, opportunities and resources. I finally felt challenged. I finally felt able to learn about things that were important, that mattered to me. Secondary school had felt so binding; university made me feel like I had choice.

Katrina, University of Toronto, Art History '04

---

2. Planning Ahead

The first few weeks of term are exceptionally busy for all students, and can be overwhelming for those in first year. The last thing you want is to be distracted by all the "administrivia" that could have been dealt with ahead of time. Be prepared by doing some advance planning during the months leading up to the beginning of term. When you realize how many demands there are on your time during those first few weeks, you will be glad you did. The first part of this chapter deals with the things you need to do to keep your personal life organized. The second part of this chapter addresses things you can do before university commences to keep your academic life organized.

Use the Planning Ahead Checklist in your *University Matters Student Planner* or download one from www.universitymatters.ca.

2.1   Banking arrangements

There is a good chance a financial institution has made a deal with your university to place Automated Teller Machines (ATMs) on campus. These are also known as Automated Banking Machines (ABMs). There may also be a bank branch on campus. In the best-case scenario, details of which financial institution this is and the services it offers will be provided to you with your registration materials, or will be disclosed on the university Web site. If not, call the university to clarify.

- If you currently have accounts with that financial institution, or are prepared to open an account there, then you are in good shape;
- If there is no bank presence on campus, or if you prefer another bank, you can use the bank Web sites to search for a branch that is convenient to your campus:
  - » The following bank Web sites have a link to a branch and/or ATM/ABM locator right on the front page:
    www.scotiabank.com
    www.cibc.com/ca/personal.html
    www.tdcanadatrust.com
  - » The National Bank of Canada also has a branch locator on its front page, under the link "Find Us." Their Web site is www.nbc.ca
  - » For the Royal Bank, go to www.rbcroyalbank.com and click on "Go to Personal Banking" where there is a link called "Branch and ATM Locator";
  - » For the Bank of Montreal, go to www.bmo.com and click on "Personal Finances" where there is a link called "ABM Branch Locator";
  - » To relate the branch addresses to the location of your campus, use www.mapquest.com or http://maps.google.ca
  - » President's Choice Financial service offers the no-fee bank account with free cheques and chequing, plus free transactions at over 4,100 President's Choice Financial, CIBC and CIBC/Amicus bank machines. Banking services for President's Choice Financial services are provided by CIBC. www.pcfinancial.ca

» Most of the other banks have special student account arrangements with reduced fees, details of which can be found on their respective Web sites:
www.cibc.com/studentlife
www.tdcanadatrust.com/student
www.rbcroyalbank.com/student
www.scotiabank.com/cda/content/0,1608,CID521_LIDen,00.html
www4.bmo.com/personal/0,4344,35649_36829,00.html

- Open a chequing account *and* a joint account with a parent.
- On-line transfers between accounts in the same financial institutions are usually instantaneous.
- Get a debit card.

If you are transferring money between financial institutions, rather than between accounts within the same bank, there can be a one- or two-day delay in receipt of funds. Find out from your bank if there is a delay, and how long it is, so you can make sure transfers to your daily banking account arrive before you run out of cash.

A joint account is helpful for unforeseen emergencies. Your parents can transfer money into the joint account from their account, using the Web if they are set up for this. If you prefer the security and privacy of operating on a day-to-day basis out of an account that is exclusively yours, immediately transfer the money out of the joint account into your own personal account.

- This arrangement is very handy if you run out of cash and need some in a hurry. With Web-based banking, your parents can refill your coffers before your "emergency" phone call to them is over.
- Have you ever heard of needing cash "not in a hurry"?

At the beginning of term you may have savings in an account that you will deplete over the year. Although interest rates are currently very low, it is still worthwhile to take steps to maximize the interest earned on these funds. Every little bit helps.

- Ask your bank what rate they pay on savings accounts.
- Consider investing in short-term Guaranteed Investment Certificates (GICs), which tend to offer higher interest rates than savings accounts. If you do this, stagger the maturities[6] of the GICs you invest in to approximately match the cash requirements indicated by your budget. For example, in early September

after paying your first tuition instalment and buying your books you may wish to invest your savings as follows:

GIC Term	Maturity	Amount	Expenses to be covered
1 month	October 1	$1000	October living expenses
2 months	November 1	$1000	November living expenses
3 months	December 1	$1000	December living expenses
4 months	January 2	$4500	January living expenses, books and tuition
5 months	February 1	$1000	February living expenses
6 months	March 1	$1000	March living expenses
7 months	April 1	$1000	April living expenses

- Canada's six major banks tend to offer very similar rates on short-term GICs. Often you will find that President's Choice Financial and ING Bank of Canada offer significantly more attractive terms on their savings accounts.[7] Even if you are not doing your daily banking with these institutions, you should consider investing your excess cash with them to maximize your interest income. Each month, you can simply go on-line and transfer cash from your savings account in one bank to your daily banking account in another bank. www.ingcanada.ca www.pcfinancial.ca

- A representative at your bank may suggest mutual funds for your savings. Funds that invest in equities or in bonds with longer maturities (more than three years) are more volatile than you should consider given the short time horizon that you are at university. You cannot afford to lose one dollar of your savings. Money market funds are a reasonable alternative, but in essence you are paying the mutual fund provider, sometimes your own bank, a fee to invest on your behalf in instruments that are very much like the GICs you can invest in yourself. It is easier and more profitable to put your money

---

6   The GICs that offer you a worthwhile interest rate advantage require you to invest your money for a fixed period of time. In other words, once you put the money in, you can't get it back out until the term of the arrangement is over. The date on which the financial institution returns the money to you is the maturity date of the GIC. In some cases you may be able to cash in a GIC before maturity, but you may have to forgo some or all of the interest you have earned.

7   The deposits and GICs of many financial institutions in Canada, including those identified above, are insured by the Canada Deposit Insurance Corporation, a crown corporation, subject to the maximum coverage limitations outlined at http://www.cdic.ca/?id=62&contid=30&count=1. If an insured institution fails, and is unable to repay to you all or part of an insured deposit, CDIC will do so instead, again subject to maximum coverage limitations.

in a high-rate savings account or buy GICs yourself.

- If you are inexperienced at budgeting, ask your parents to allocate money monthly from your savings account to your joint account until you have learned how to budget:[8]
  - » If you haven't managed cash inflows and outflows, don't expect to be good at it right away. As is the case with a lot of things in life, you will get better with practice.

2.2   Financial assistance

Financial assistance is available in two forms:

- An award, such as a scholarship or bursary, which does not need to be repaid;
- A loan from the government or a financial institution, which has to be repaid after graduation.

Many programs for financial assistance are based on financial need.

- To determine eligibility for such programs you need to prepare an estimate of your expenses, and the amount of money you have available. If you have too little money to meet your expenses then you are in financial need and may qualify for needs-based programs like student support bursaries.
- Your parents' income will likely be taken into consideration whether or not they are prepared to provide you with financial assistance.
- Refer to Chapter 15 and download the Budgeting Spreadsheet from www.universitymatters.ca

Fifty-one percent of undergraduate students report having an average of $13,201 of debt resulting from financing their university education. The sample from which this average was taken includes students in all years of undergraduate programs; those further along in their programs typically owe more.[9]

Contact your university's awards office to get information on scholarships and bursaries. Also check these Web sites:

www.studentawards.com

---

8   To do this you will have to make your savings account joint with at least one of your parents, which means that they will have unrestricted access to your money. In the rare cases where the parents are worse at budgeting than you, or you are uncomfortable with providing this access, then this is not a viable option and must be avoided.

9   Survey of Undergraduate University Students: University of Winnipeg, 2002, downloaded from http://www.uwinnipeg.ca/index/cms-filesystem-action?file=pdfs/future/cusc.pdf on April 6, 2005.

www.scholarshipscanada.com
www.aucc.ca
www.myschool101.com
www.schoolfinder.com

Some university scholarships are awarded based on
academic merit and are offered automatically with
your acceptance letter. You need to apply for others.

Many scholarships go unclaimed so take the time to apply for them if you meet the eligibility requirements. In some cases only a few applicants come forward, so there is a good chance of coming out on top.

- Certain scholarships are awarded solely on
  academic achievement, but others consider
  community involvement, participation in
  sports, ethnic background, leadership, innovation and family affiliations.
- Ask your parents to check with their employers and unions to see if any
  scholarships are available to support university education.
- Remember to send a thank you note for any awards you receive.

Bursaries are awarded based on financial need. First, you have to apply for government-sponsored loans and then submit a detailed budget showing the need for
additional financial assistance. Bursaries do not need to be repaid.

- Students who apply for financial aid from the province or territory in which
  they reside are automatically considered for a bursary from the Canadian
  Millennium Scholarship Fund:
  www.millenniumscholarships.ca

Explore government-funded financial aid programs.

- The federal government assists students via the Canada Student Loans
  Program. Full details are on this site:
  www.hrsdc.gc.ca/en/gateways/nav/top_nav/program/cslp.shtml
- Each province has its own loans program. Details of each are available on the
  following sites:
  www.campusaccess.com
  www.canlearn.ca

In 2002-2003, **94,256** Canadian Millennium Scholarships
were awarded totalling over **$288 million**.

Government-sponsored student loan programs are intended to cover up to 60 percent of your assessed needs. If you do not have sufficient savings or other financial

assistance to cover the balance, you may need to consider a standby line of credit with your bank. Details of each bank's student loan programs can be found on their respective Web sites as detailed in Chapter 2.1.

- You should expect to pay competitive interest rates at a spread of 1 to 2 percent over Prime.[10]
- The bank may insist that a third party, someone with a sufficiently strong credit rating, such as a parent, guarantee your loan.
- A standby line of credit may provide peace of mind, but try not to think of it as a ready source of spending money.
- If you have a bank loan, a monthly statement will be mailed to you showing the loan balance and the interest that is due on the outstanding debt.

If you borrow under the student loan plans offered by banks, the bank will typically charge you interest while you are at school and require you to pay it on a monthly basis.

If you obtain a student loan under the Canada Student Loans Program, the federal government covers the cost of interest while you are at school.

Both forms of loans typically do not require repayment of principal until at least six months after graduation.

- CIBC's Web site presents an excellent guidebook for university and college students, which lays out the similarities and differences between government loans and bank loans: www.cibc.com/ca/pdf/student-workbook-en.pdf

You may qualify for a work-study position that is available on campus for students who are unable to obtain sufficient loans to cover their expenses. These positions are limited, so inquire early.

If you think you might run short of funds, ask your family for a loan. To increase their comfort level, work out a specific repayment plan. You might be able to repay them with funds from your tax refund. Refer to Chapter 15.4 for more details.

2.3   Get a health tune-up

Your physician. Make an appointment with your doctor for a full annual physical examination a month or two before university commences.

---

10   A bank's Prime rate is the interest rate it charges to its best and most creditworthy customers. The rate fluctuates with the Bank of Canada's decision to raise or lower short-term lending rates.

- If you have any health issues that require ongoing monitoring, ask your doctor for a referral to a doctor in your university town. Ask your doctor to forward a copy of your medical records to the new doctor.
- Some medical conditions entitle you to specific accommodations at university, such as extra time to write exams, a room to yourself to write exams, or specially adapted technological support. See also Chapter 3.7. Obtain a note from your doctor attesting to your condition so it is available to present if the university so requires. To find out the situations for which the universities make accommodations, do the following:
  » Talk to your doctor about your condition and ask if he or she thinks your condition warrants specific accommodations, or if he or she is aware that accommodations are typically made in cases like yours;
  » Determine either from the material the university sends to you or publishes on its Web site, or by making inquiries, what the university's policies are with regard to students with disabilities.

Five percent of students report having a disability.[11]

- If you are female, consult with your doctor about an annual pap smear if you are or have been sexually active.
- Tell your doctor about any hearing problems you may have experienced. Ask your doctor to examine your ears. If the hearing problems you specify are sufficiently serious, or if he or she detects an unusual level of wax buildup or other abnormality, he or she may refer you to an ear, nose and throat specialist. Increasingly, students are discovering that they have undetected hearing loss. Your ability to hear well at university is important. You may not be able to sit near the professor in class, and you will likely find yourself talking and listening in group situations, both of which will challenge your ability to hear.
- Obtain prescription drug renewals, including birth control pills, with enough repeats for the year ahead. If you are going out of province, the easiest thing to do is fill your prescriptions before you leave home, to the extent you can. If you explain your situation to your doctor, he or she may be able to make the order quantities large enough to cover you between trips home. If not,

It is not always possible to fill a prescription issued in one province at a pharmacy in a second province. Some pharmacies will only fill prescriptions issued in their home province, or may limit you to the initial order, and decline to provide refills.

---

11   Survey of Undergraduate University Students: University of Winnipeg, 2002, downloaded from http://www.uwinnipeg.ca/index/cms-filesystem-action?file=pdfs/future/cusc.pdf on April 6, 2005.

make a plan with a parent, relative or friend to fill repeats from your usual pharmacy, and have them shipped to you.

- Discuss the following immunizations with your doctor:
  - » A tetanus booster shot if you haven't had one recently. This vaccination is recommended every 10 years, and protects against tetanus, which is also known as lockjaw. If you cut yourself or step on a nail, you will have saved yourself a visit to the emergency room for a tetanus shot;
  - » A vaccine called menjugate will immunize you against Neisseria Meningitis group C. This protects you from a rare but very severe type of meningitis, which is most common in teenagers and university students. Some provincial health plans provide it to certain age groups as a matter of course; otherwise, ask your doctor about it, and if it is right for you, he or she will provide a prescription and, in most cases, arrange to administer it. The vaccine costs about $120. As a student, you may be able to obtain it under a parent's medical insurance plan;
  - » If you have not been immunized against Hepatitis B, you should arrange this as well. Hepatitis B is the only sexually transmitted infection that can be prevented with immunization.

Your dentist. Make an appointment for a checkup and ask for a referral to a dentist in your university town for emergencies.

- As a full-time student you will be covered automatically under university health and dental group plans with premium charges added to student fees.
- You may be covered for medical and dental expenses under your parents' plans while you are in full-time attendance at school.

If you are covered under a parent's plan, you may be able to "opt-out" of medical and dental insurance fees that are included in university "activity fees" and receive a partial rebate. Inquire at your university. Be prepared to provide proof of coverage and don't miss the opt-out deadline!

- Ask your parents to confirm with their insurer what they need to do to ensure their plan continues to cover you, especially when you turn twenty-one while at university. Parents will have to provide proof that you are registered as a full-time student, so obtain the document they need to do so.
- Before opting out of the university insurance coverage, estimate your personal medical and dental needs for the coming year:
  - » If each of your parents has a plan, you will likely be able to cover 100 percent of eligible claims;
  - » If only one parent has a plan that covers 80 percent of your claims and if you require ongoing expensive treatment, you may be wise to maintain the university insurance to reimburse you for the additional 20 percent of your claims.

Your ophthalmologist/optometrist. Have your eyes tested and, if you already have prescription lenses, confirm that the prescription is still correct.

- In almost all first-year courses, and in many upper year courses, the classrooms will be large enough to make it difficult for you to see the screen or blackboard at the front. Quite a few first-year courses are held in auditoriums, so the distance to the front of the room can be substantial. If your eyes are less-than-perfect, you will definitely need your glasses or contact lenses. Also, it can be very tiring to work in a lecture and note-taking environment if you are struggling with imperfect vision.
- Losing or breaking glasses while at university can be a major inconvenience. Obtain a copy of your prescription; write down the model number of your frames, and the name of the retailer that sold them to you. Armed with this information, you won't have much difficulty finding replacements, sometimes even from the same retail chain as in your hometown.

2.4 Other health matters

Most universities offer medical services through a campus health service, since local doctors often don't want to have to deal with transient patients. Check to see the extent of services offered by your university.

- Ensure you have your provincial medical card in your possession and that it is current. Some cards now have expiry dates. Check to see if it will require renewal in the school year ahead. If so, obtain and complete the paperwork now.
  - » If you are going to a different province to study, take your health insurance card with you;

» Contact your provincial health agency to inform them that you will be studying outside of the province, or your health coverage may be cancelled;

» If you are from Alberta, you will need to pay the health care premium charged in that province. If you are a student moving to Alberta from another province to attend university, you remain covered by your home province;

» All of the provinces, with the exception of Quebec, have entered into reciprocal arrangements. In these provinces, you are allowed to submit your provincial health insurance card and obtain full coverage.

If your permanent residence is in Quebec and you are studying out of province, be prepared to pay cash for medical visits and to seek reimbursement from the Quebec provincial government afterwards.

Some universities, especially those close to the Quebec border, will accept the Quebec health insurance card and absorb the difference. Check with Health Services at your university.

If you are studying in Quebec and are from another province, check coverage arrangements with Health Services at your university.

Consider enrolling in a local First Aid CPR course so that you can be ready to help others in an emergency situation. This is important lifelong knowledge. www.epa-cpr.com

Familiarize yourself with ergonomics to ensure you are seated comfortably when studying and typing in order to avoid repetitive strain injuries, such as Carpal Tunnel Syndrome (CTS). Your wrists should be in line with your elbows, and your

A typical undergraduate spends 17 hours per week on the computer.[12]

upper arms should be relaxed at your sides when typing. Be aware of early warning signs such as pains in your wrists, shoulders and neck. The sooner you seek help the easier the strain is to treat. The recovery from injury can be slow. These types of injuries can severely affect your ability to produce written work.

• For more details on ergonomics and CTS refer to: www.ctsplace.com
• For some preventive stretch exercises refer to: www.mydailyyoga.com/yoga/rsi.html

---

12   Survey of Undergraduate University Students: University of Winnipeg, 2002, downloaded from http://www.uwinnipeg.ca/index/cms-filesystem-action?file=pdfs/future/cusc.pdf on April 6, 2005.

- If you tend to cradle the phone between your ear and shoulder, you might be vulnerable to a strain injury. Avoid having this occur at university by breaking the habit now. If you tend to be on the phone for prolonged periods of time, obtain a headset.
- Invest in a strong backpack that centres the weight of heavy books across your body. There are several good choices including those made by ObusForme, but be sure to spend time trying them out before buying one. Avoid carrying a heavy backpack across one shoulder or in one hand, or you may suffer injuries.

2.5   Accommodation

There are a number of alternatives to consider when deciding upon the accommodation that is right for you. The major alternatives are:
- Staying at home, or with relatives or family friends in a family home situation; and
- The independent arrangements:
  » Residence;
  » Living alone or with one or more roommates of the same gender;
  » Living in a coed situation.
- Think about which is right for you; find out what other university students have experienced.
- Consider your Personal Goals Worksheet in your *University Matters Student Planner* and downloadable from www.universitymatters.ca, and think about which alternative fits best with what is important to you.
- Look at the What to Take With You Checklist and the House Rules Checklist in your *University Matters Student Planner* and downloadable from www.universitymatters.ca to give you an idea of some of the issues associated with living in your own house, and with roommates.

If you are applying for residence, consider the following:
- Residence quality often varies significantly, ranging from spacious and bright rooms in the newer buildings to smaller, pokier rooms in the older buildings.

Set your expectations based on the latter. If you luck out and end up in a great room, consider it a bonus. Universities will sometimes conduct their tours through the better residences, so again, set your expectations based on a realistic outcome rather than on what you see on such tours.

- Fill out the residence application form in detail, and review Appendix 2, House Rules, to identify habits you could not tolerate in a roommate; if there are some, state them clearly on the application form.

- Ask for the contact information of your roommate. Make contact during the summer so you can get to know each other before arriving on campus. You can also coordinate sharing items such as a mini-fridge.

- **Forty-six percent** of students live either in a rented space or a home they own.
- Forty percent live at home with their parents or other relatives.
- Fourteen percent of first-year students report living in residence.[13]

Arrange your living accommodation well before the term commences.

- Many leases run from May to May so students already at university make their arrangement in February and March. By April, much of the trading of apartments back and forth is already finished.

Finding pleasant accommodation that is affordable can be a discouraging process, so be prepared to reduce your expectations.

- The university's housing information site will probably be available on-line.
- Ask Student Services about the local community and whether there are any areas that are considered unsafe or undesirable.
- Use the Internet to search the classified section of local papers of the city you are moving to.
- Set aside a weekend to visit your new community and secure housing.
  - » When you are looking, the competition for a "decent place" could be intense;
  - » There could be groups of people lined up outside a house or apartment as you inspect it, ready to take it if you turn it down;
  - » If you want to commit to a particular place, you will have to provide a deposit on the spot;

---

13   Survey of Undergraduate University Students: University of Winnipeg, 2002, downloaded from http://www.uwinnipeg.ca/index/cms-filesystem-action?file=pdfs/future/cusc.pdf on April 6, 2005.

» The landlord will probably take a cheque, but you need a backup plan in case he or she insists on cash;

» A reasonable backup plan involves carrying some cash and a debit card. Offer to get the cash from the bank and return with it within a specific time frame. The landlord may ask for some cash to ensure you return. This is what your cash holdings are for. Debit card withdrawals usually have a daily limit, which could fall short of the usual deposit—one month's rent. If so, you need to carry cash equal to the difference between your estimate of one month's rent and your daily withdrawal limit;

» When you make a deposit, get a receipt and the contact details of the person you gave it to, especially for a cash deposit. Ask to see photo identification (e.g., a driver's licence) and record the details (e.g., the driver's licence number).

- If you are renting and the walls are a little shabby, the landlord may be prepared to supply paint and materials in exchange for your labour. If possible, plan to paint before moving in.

Refer to Chapter 14.3 if you are going to be sharing your living space so that you can avoid "the nightmare roommate."

Review the landlord and tenant rights for the province in which you will be living.
- The Student Housing office or the Legal Aid office will likely have this information available for you.
- Verify whether the landlord can ask for first and last month's rent or a damage deposit. You may be entitled to receive interest on your last month's deposit.
- If the landlord makes any promises, get them in writing as soon as possible, preferably on the spot.
- Take photographs of any damage and ask the landlord to acknowledge them so that you are not blamed for such damage at a later date.

Understand your lease.
- Under joint tenancy, each tenant is responsible for the entire amount of the rent. If one or more of your roommates fails to pay his or her share, the rest of the roomates are responsible for it.
- Under tenancy in common, each roommate is a separate tenant who is only responsible for his or her share of the rent.
- Determine how much notice you are required to give to terminate the lease.
- For easy reference, file a copy of your lease in your "House Info" folder as suggested in Chapter 5.4.

Arrange tenant's home insurance.

Familiarize yourself with fire safety rules before leaving home.
- Buy a fire extinguisher to take with you. Read the instructions carefully and make sure you and all of your housemates know how to use it. Your first shopping trip after moving in should include baking soda, which can put out a small fire. When you move in, put the fire extinguisher and the baking soda in a readily accessible location. Make sure everyone in the house is aware of the location.
- If you have doubts about the smoke and CO detectors, or they are missing, buy your own. They are very cheap in comparison to what can happen if they fail or are absent. This makes a nice going-away gift for you, so drop the hint with your parents. As parents, we can assure you, you don't even have to be subtle on this one!
- If you choose to rely on smoke and CO detectors in place, put in brand new batteries! Follow the manufacturers' instructions for testing them at the outset. Follow the manufacturers' protocols for periodic testing. If the instructions are absent, buy some new detectors.

Be prepared to wait three or four weeks for telephone installation, whether you are in residence or in your own place. The beginning of term can be stressful and disorienting, and is a time when you might need to call home to obtain the support of your family and friends. Lining up at a pay phone in this situation, or going without, can be discouraging and frustrating. Consider whether you should obtain a cell phone to cover off your needs until a land line is installed.

2.6　What to take with you

As you get ready to move, whether into residence or other accommodation, plan ahead for the basic comforts in life.

- Use the What to Take With You Checklist in Appendix 1 or download a copy from www.universitymatters.ca. A copy can also be found in your *University Matters Student Planner.*
- Observe what you use at home for a week or two and add to the list as necessary.
- If you are moving into a rental property, ensure you have lots of cleaning materials when you arrive.
- Check what the landlord or university residence provides with your accommodation.
- Scrounge whatever furniture you can from home, family and friends.
- Willingly accept second-hand items that are in good shape. You can get fussy and replace them at a later date when you have the spare cash! Post notes in grocery stores saying you are a student and indicate the pieces you need. Often someone is looking for an opportunity to pass on certain items that they no longer need but which are still in good condition.
- Scour yard sales and let the vendors know you are a poor student on a tight budget. Leave your phone number with them in case they don't sell everything and will look to you to take stuff off their hands at the end of the day.
- Request items you need from family members for your birthday or on other gift occasions.
- For most kitchen supplies, the dollar store is a great place. You can get spatulas, wooden spoons, measuring cups and spoons…all the little things you may not need right away, but might want as you become more adventurous with your cooking.
- If you are going to be cooking your own meals, get familiar with the prices of food you enjoy. Read the flyers that the grocery stores include in the daily newspaper and learn to recognize the sale prices. For instance, why pay $1.09 for a box of Kraft Dinner when it often goes on sale for 69¢ and sometimes even two for 99¢. If transportation is not an issue, you should stock up on sale-priced staples during the summer.
- Visit your local bulk food outlet and stock up on spices, herbs and other staples before you leave.

If you are moving to a university that is far from your hometown, it probably isn't feasible to purchase everything you need before you leave home. In this situation, plan to get to your new residence a few days before orientation starts to allow time for shopping.

- If your parents are driving you to university, plan to spend an afternoon with your list in hand buying all that you need.
- This is also an opportunity for your parents to help you stock your freezer and cupboards with staples and paper products.

Make a list of EVERYTHING you need for your new place, then take a trip to Zellers or WalMart or some other ridiculously complete big box store. Take the bus there and then, once you're all loaded up with everything you could possibly need, take a taxi back. The most this will cost you is maybe $30, and the cost is minimized if you're taking the trip with roommates. If you do it right and really stock up on laundry detergent and toilet paper, you'll never have to mess with the awkwardness of carrying something large home on the bus.

Nora, McGill University, Engineering '06

A lot of people who graduated in May sell off their belongings to incoming students in September. While looking for used books signs, keep an eye out for used furniture and kitchen supply signs as well.

Queen's started relatively late in comparison with other universities, and so most of my friends had already spent a week or so in classes, while I was still in the throes of packing. I talked with a lot of them during this time, asking them how classes were going, how they were finding res life, and things like that. I also started asking them if there was anything they forgot that I should bring with me. A lot of my friends told me to bring snack foods. One friend said she wished she had brought bed raisers for added storage under her bed. Someone else told me to bring lots of extra power cords. Then I talked to my friend Tom. He thought for a little while when I asked him if there was anything he forgot, and then he responded. He said to me, "I would recommend bringing paper and pens. Yeah, that's what I forgot. My roommate forgot too. But it's ok. We borrowed some from the girl across the hall. Eventually though, I'm going to have to buy my own." I laughed for quite a while after he said that to me. I guess some people take packing a little more seriously than others, but it seemed to all work out!

Zoe, Queen's University, ArtSci '08

2.7   Getting organized

Ideally, you should obtain your *University Matters Student Planner* available from www.universitymatters.ca shortly after high school ends. Start using it as soon as you get it—no need to wait until university commences. The more you have practiced using it, the more proficient you will be with it when your hectic first term starts. Also, the sooner you start using it, the sooner your *University Matters Student Planner* will begin capturing the events and commitments that are important in your life, and the more complete it will be. Chapter 5.3 describes some typical entries you can make in the month or two before term starts.

- Update your resume if you intend to look for a part-time job during the term. Ask previous employers for reference letters with their contact information. Make copies and take them with you. Don't forget to get reference letters for any babysitting jobs you have done if you intend to look for child care jobs in your new location.

- Arrange to reroute mail normally sent to your address at home such as magazines, and bank statements. How you do this depends on how frequently you expect to change addresses at university.

  » It takes time and effort to submit change-of-address forms to the parties who send mail to you. Also, there can be long and variable lag times between submitting the change and having it put into effect, so it is difficult to know when the change of address will start.

  » If you plan to live at the same address for the duration of university, then changing your address with the parties who send mail to you is probably worthwhile and effective.

  » If, like most university students, you think you will change addresses at university several times, then arrange with Canada Post to redirect your mail from your home address to your university address. Under a redirection of mail, the issuers of mail continue to use your home address. The post office reroutes it to your university address. Implementing a redirection requires completion of a single form at the post office, and it can be set up to start and end on specific dates.

- Make two photocopies of all the cards you carry in your wallet. Refrain from writing down any PIN numbers. Keep a copy in a place that is safe and accessible to you at university. Leave a copy with your parents. The copied information will be very helpful if you lose a card or if one gets stolen.

- Buy an accordion file and plenty of manila folders. Set up a personal filing system as suggested in Chapter 5.4. You need to have this ready, as the paper flow is about to begin. You will find it easy to stay organized if you have a proper home for all the documents that will be coming your way.

Purchase a roll of sticky labels (3" by 1.25" ought to do it) and use them to cover over the titles on used manila folders. This enables you to reuse manila folders over and over again, saving you money and helping the environment. Perhaps more importantly, it increases the chances of having a usable folder on hand when you need it, helping you stay organized.

- If you require parking, inquire well before arriving on campus. Campuses are characterized by a large number of students, staff, faculty and visitors descending daily on a relatively small geographic area. Although there are exceptions, it is typically difficult to make a campus work in a car-oriented culture. This is all the more so for an urban campus. For the typical university, long-term committed spots are difficult and expensive to obtain, street parking on or near campus can be a nightmare of arcane "limited parking" or "no parking" rules, and parking monitors are vigilant. If you can avoid depending on a car to get you to campus, do so unless you can afford it and have determined that your campus is "car friendly."

Sixty-three percent of students are dissatisfied or very dissatisfied with parking facilities at their university.[14]

- Explore the local transportation routes and inquire whether student passes are available. You will need student identification and probably a recent photo. Student Services can probably advise you on this as well.
- Find out if you need to provide a photograph of yourself for your student ID card. If you do, determine the photo specifications and follow the instructions provided. Arrange to mail or e-mail your photo before arriving on campus if so instructed.
- Contact the athletic department early in the summer if you are a keen athlete and would like to join a varsity team.

---

14   Survey of Undergraduate University Students: University of Winnipeg, 2002, downloaded from http://www.uwinnipeg.ca/index/cms-filesystem-action?file=pdfs/future/cusc.pdf on April 6, 2005.

- » If you are already a member of another nearby athletic facility and do not wish to use the campus facilities, you may be able to opt-out of the portion of fees charged for athletics. Check with your university.
- Take advantage of your university's e-mail system and establish an account as soon as they will let you, before arriving on campus if the university is willing.
  - » E-mail your new address to all your friends and family so they can easily keep in touch with you. If your account isn't going live right away, tell them the start date. This will be one less thing you need to think about as you start classes.
- Arrange child care well in advance. Your university may have a child care centre with limited space available, so register on the waiting list as soon as possible. Arrange emergency backup in the event your regular provider is sick.

> **About eight** percent of undergraduate students report having children.[15]

2.8 Getting ready to learn

Surf your university's Web site and check out the extent of computer lab facilities.
- Give serious thought to whether you need your own computer. On-campus computer labs have numerous computers, but they might not be available when you need them. If you are not well-organized and tend to leave your papers until close to the due date, you may be extremely frustrated as you watch other students checking their e-mail or surfing the Internet while the hours you have left to complete your paper tick away.
  - » Check out the lease and purchase plans that your university offers through Computer Services or the bookstore.
  - » Arrange your student computing account ahead of time if you can.
- Most students today are excellent word processors thanks to MSN. If you are not, practice your typing skills and consider buying one of the many touch-typing training software products that are available. Get up to speed before September. The increase in efficiency will be very helpful.

> **Your parents** might be able to purchase a second-hand computer that is in excellent shape from their employer's IT department.

---

15 Survey of Undergraduate University Students: University of Winnipeg, 2002, downloaded from http://www.uwinnipeg.ca/index/cms-filesystem-action?file=pdfs/future/cusc.pdf on April 6, 2005.

- » Inquire about what software is usually used in your academic program and ensure your computer skills are current, e.g., Word, Excel and PowerPoint.
- Consider a math or writing refresher course if your skills are weak in either of these areas.
  - » Some universities offer a prep week prior to "frosh"[16] week, in which various academic workshops are offered. Inquire about them and register as soon as you can to make sure you secure a place.
  - » You are better off to spend time on fundamentals before classes start because you will need to focus your time on assigned work during the term.
- Ask an academic advisor whether there are any recommended support books. There are specialized dictionaries for different subject areas. A good bookstore or the campus bookstore will have a selection.
  - » For mathematics there is *The HarperCollins Dictionary of Mathematics* by E. J. Borowski and J. M. Borwein (ISBN 0064610195).
  - » Writing handbooks include:
    - » *Making Sense: A student's guide to writing and style* by Margot Northey (ISBN 0195404270);
    - » *Making Sense: A Student's Guide to Research and Writing* by Margot Northey and David B. Knight (ISBN 0195415272);
    - » *The Elements of Style* by William Strunk Jr. and E. B. White (ISBN 0-205-30902-X).
    - » For research essays, there is *The Research Essay: A Guide to Essays and Papers* by Hugh Robertson (ISBN 0969306873).
    - » It is helpful to have more than one writing handbook to get better coverage and alternate explanations of complicated topics.

Go to a local library or that of a nearby college or university and familiarize yourself with the current technologies for finding articles and books.
- Once on campus, if you can find the books and articles you need efficiently, the time you save can go to writing a better paper.
- Your university will probably have an on-line link to the library's Web site. If so, explore the databases for your field of study. Learning how to use this resource ahead of time will save you time when you are doing your research.
  - » Some universities have developed on-line courses to teach students how

---

16   Frosh is the shortened version of freshman referring to a first-year student, or more generally a new-comer.

to use the library's resources. Take advantage of this before you arrive on campus.

2.9 The calendar—a "contract" between you and the university

The requirements of each degree program, along with information concerning admission, academic regulations, fees and much more, are set out in a document called a calendar. At some universities each faculty has its own calendar. At others there is a single calendar for all undergraduate programs.

- The calendar is the governing document for most of your relationship with the university. In a sense, it operates like a contract between you and the university concerning your degree. You need to read it to determine your exact program requirements and the rules and regulations to which you will be subject.
- Familiarize yourself with the calendar so you understand your program's requirements and the manner in which course prerequisites are structured. This topic is addressed in Chapter 2.10.
- The calendar sets out your university's academic rules and regulations. The calendar also defines what constitutes things like an academic offence and academic dishonesty. It is important to understand these as all Canadian universities take them seriously and enforce them. The standards at university may very well be different from what you are used to.

The definition of academic dishonesty that Queen's University uses:
- *Academic dishonesty* is broadly understood as any action that undermines the academic integrity of the Faculty and/or the University. Academic dishonesty includes plagiarism as well as any deliberate attempt to gain unfair advantage academically for oneself or others. Dishonest practices include fabrication of data, cheating, or the uttering of false statements relating to academic work by a student.[17]

Read your university's definition of plagiarism and digest the content. Plagiarism guidelines are strictly enforced. In addition to appearing in the calendar, they are probably spelled out on-line and in course outlines.

---

17   From Queen's University's Faculty of Arts and Science Calendar for the academic year 2004-2005, downloaded from http://www.queensu.ca/calendars/artsci/TextOnly/Regulation12_ _ _AcademicDishonesty and FailuretoAbidebyAcademicRules_2391.htm April 20, 2005.

- To avoid plagiarism, learn how to cite material and document your sources.

Most writing handbooks address this topic. Familiarize yourself with the citation style used in your field. Being familiar with the commonly used citation styles will help you understand what your professor wants:[19]

  » APA is used for papers in psychology, education and other social sciences [c.f. *APA Citation Style, Publication Manual of the American Psychological Association*, 5th edition or www.apastyle.org];

  » MLA is used in literature, arts, and humanities [c.f. *MLA Citation Style MLA Handbook for Writers of Research Papers*, 6th edition or http://webster.commnet.edu/mla/index.shtml];

  » AMA is used in medicine, health, and biological sciences [c.f. *American Medical Association Manual of Style*, 9th ed., 1998];

  » Turabian is used for college or university papers on a variety of subjects [c.f. *Turabian Citation Style, A Manual for Writers of Term Papers, Theses, and Dissertations*, 6th edition];

  » Chicago is used in the popular press [c.f. *Chicago Citation Style The Chicago Manual of Style*, 15th edition].

You can get zero on an essay for "lifting" material without appropriate references. You may fail the course automatically or be suspended from university even though you genuinely did not intend to "cheat." Avoid this life lesson!

- Borrowing someone else's answers and using them to help you prepare your own is very likely an academic offence. Unauthorized possession of tests or answers to tests might also be academic offences.
- Do not submit essentially the same essay to different courses.
- Sometimes students are asked to work in a group but each member is expected to submit an individual report. Although you are allowed to benefit

---

18 From Queen's University's Faculty of Arts and Science Calendar for the academic year 2004-2005, downloaded from http://www.queensu.ca/calendars/artsci/TextOnly/Regulation12_ _ _AcademicDishonesty andFailuretoAbidebyAcademicRules_2391.htm April 20, 2005.
19 Once your classes start and professors begin assigning papers, they will probably indicate the style they prefer. If they don't, ask them before you begin writing the paper. It is much more time-efficient to begin with and follow the correct style than it is to fix up a paper that has been completed using an incorrect style.

> **Do not lend** your work "as a guide" to anyone. There have been lots of cases in which a student has shown his or her work to another student because the friend says he or she "just needs to get an indication of what is required," only to find out later that the friend has copied entire sections into his or her paper and submitted it as original work. The university cannot tell whose work came first. Often both parties are penalized.

from the research and work done by others you are expected to summarize it yourself. Write your submission in your own words unless instructed otherwise by the professor.

- Software is now available that enables professors to compare your report to an Internet database and highlights all the sections that have been "borrowed" from various articles and papers. If you have not properly attributed the work of others, you will be in trouble!

2.10   Course selection

As a high school student you were probably used to being handed your schedule. Now you have to organize lectures along with tutorials and labs to fulfill your program requirements.

- Course selection can be a complex interplay of a number of factors, including your interests, your program's requirements, whether courses are being offered during the term in which you need them, and whether you can find a combination of time slots that avoids scheduling overlaps. On larger campuses it is prudent to check whether courses scheduled back to back are near enough to one another to enable you to walk from one to the other in the usual ten minutes scheduled for this.

- Many universities offer academic advisory sessions during the summer to help you select the correct courses to match your interests and program requirements.

  » The majority of students tend to ignore these opportunities because of work commitments, travel challenges or simply because they don't want to leave the cottage;

  » Those students who do take advantage of these sessions find them very helpful;

  » Use academic advisors and listen to them. Faculties or departments often have academic advisors who can talk to you about your program and the course sequencing that will enable you to get what you want, when you want it.

- Plan your schedule well in advance of registration.
  - » Refer to your program's handbook or to the university calendar to determine the core courses you need to register for and the number of electives you can consider;
  - » Most full-time students take four or five courses each term, which translates into about fifteen hours of class time. If you are taking science courses, you will have laboratory sessions as well;
  - » Select your first choices;
  - » Identify backup choices for each course in case your first choices are unavailable when you register.
- As mentioned in Chapter 2.9, pay close attention to prerequisite courses.
  - » If you register for a course you are not qualified to take, you may be forced to withdraw and may end up with a shortfall of courses for the term;
  - » In extreme cases, having to withdraw from a course because of the lack of a prerequisite can throw off sections of your course sequencing, extending your program by an entire term, or even a year;
  - » Find out the policy of the department from which you are taking a course since enforcement of prerequisites can vary by department;
  - » In some cases, the lack of prerequisite enforcement can give you the flexibility you need. But you must be careful. Prerequisites, even if not enforced, are there for a reason. It is usually unwise to take a course that has a specified prerequisite if you are unfamiliar with the material that is addressed in the prerequisite. The course instructor will proceed at a pace and level that assume you know the prerequisite material, which can leave you floundering.
- Popular courses are offered in numerous sections, sometimes as many as eight or ten. That is, the same course is offered more than once in a single term. It can be taught in different time slots by the same professor, or in the same time slot, but in different rooms and by different professors. This is where advance research pays off.

If you do not live near the campus, schedule a telephone appointment with an academic advisor.

Eighty-eight percent of undergraduate students are going to university full-time.[20]

---

20   Survey of Undergraduate University Students: University of Winnipeg, 2002, downloaded from http://www.uwinnipeg.ca/index/cms-filesystem-action?file=pdfs/future/cusc.pdf on April 6, 2005.

- » Read student reviews of professors if available;
- » Ask upper-year students, or your alumnus mentor if you have one, for information on a particular professor's teaching style.
- If you have the choice, be sensible by spreading your courses throughout the week.
  - » Some courses will offer lectures that are three hours long. If you have two of these in a row, you will be pretty worn out by the end of the second session and may find it difficult to maintain your concentration;
  - » On the other hand, taking three-hour courses is more efficient from a time-management and travel-time perspective, which may open up your schedule to fit in a part-time job or make a commitment to team sports;

Fewer people sign up for 8:30 a.m. classes and Thursday and Friday evening classes. Select one of these for your first choice if you anticipate the day sessions filling quickly.

- » Keep a record of your selections, and the reasons for them.
- Read course outlines ahead of time if they are posted on the university's Web site. Refer to Chapter 4.2. If the required textbooks are identified, then buy them as soon as possible to avoid long lineups and to ensure availability as campus bookstores can run out of stock. Make sure the course outline is current and applicable to the term in which you will be taking the course. Sometimes outdated course outlines remain posted, and the textbooks they specify may not be correct for the upcoming term. Refer to Chapter 3.4.

2.11 Course registration

Registration can be a frustrating process for some, so persistence is necessary.

- Register on time to ensure you have the best chance of getting the classes and schedule you want.
  - » The sooner you register, the better you will be able to manage your schedule.
- Registration is usually done via the Web. Keep trying if a course you

"On time" is not a fuzzy concept. If registration for your program opens at 9:00 a.m. on a particular day, this does not mean to register when it becomes convenient for you. It means get on the Internet or telephone at exactly 9:00 a.m. and keep trying until you are done. Don't give up!

want is full, as someone may withdraw from the course and create an opening.

- Typically you won't get much sympathy, or more importantly, adjustment, if you miss a deadline, or if a course filled up while you sat around thinking about what to do.

  » This is where the impersonal side of university can differ markedly from high school. It is not that the university staff are being insensitive. Often, many students fail to register on time for their desired courses and the staff cannot give special considerations just to you and not to the others. So, no one gets special consideration. Administrators deal with thousands of appeals to get into courses.

- If you are registering for an elective, make sure it will count toward your degree. Most programs limit how many you can take. Speak to an academic advisor if you are unsure.

- Confirm which term each course is in and whether it is a one-term course[22] or a full-year course spread over two terms. Find out if you have to register separately for each term of a full-year course.

- If you are an early bird, register for early morning courses. If you are a night owl, plan accordingly.

- After you have registered you will be able to go on-line to determine your tuition and other fees that are payable. Ensure you pay your fees on time to avoid any late charges.

- Compare the registration confirmation from the university to your record of courses you intended to select. Deal with any discrepancies promptly.

---

21 Survey of Undergraduate University Students: University of Winnipeg, 2002, downloaded from http://www.uwinnipeg.ca/index/cms-filesystem-action?file=pdfs/future/cusc.pdf on April 6, 2005.
22 Courses that span only a single term are also referred to as half-courses.

2.12   Seek input from all available resources

Ask for advice on courses, campus life and life away from home from friends, their siblings, family members, neighbours and anyone else who has been to university.

- Seek input from alumni. Your university might even have a program that will match you with an alumnus from your program so that the alumnus can act as a mentor.
- Some universities offer a "Peer Mentor" program. In this kind of program the university assigns an upper-year student to one or more First Years to answer questions and help with the adjustment to university life. Ask your Student Services advisor what programs are available.
- Surf the Web site of your university to explore all the services and opportunities that will be available to you.
- Some universities have student ambassadors profiled on their Web sites. These students are willing to share their experiences with First Years and you can benefit from their insights and tips:
  - » Don't be shy about dropping them an e-mail with questions or just to say hi. They are there to help you.

There are also volunteer groups such as Bouge, founded in early 2003. Bouge is a non-profit organization that helps high school students learn more about the opportunities available in the Canadian knowledge economy. They help students find mentors in business, governance, engineering and technology. www.bouge.ca.

- Universities will typically send you one or more packages of leaflets and booklets in the weeks before the term starts. You might feel somewhat overwhelmed by them, but try to read them all. They contain many nuggets of really useful information, and you won't have time to read them once the term starts. File them in your "University Info—Brochures" folder for later access.
- Familiarize yourself with the myriad of possible extracurricular activities that

are available, such as student associations, fraternities, sororities, clubs, volunteer work and team sports.

» A complete list of clubs and societies is likely available on the university Web site. There are hundreds of opportunities, so browse through them in the weeks before term commences and start thinking about the ones most attractive to you;

» Be wary of fraternities and sororities; they can have expensive fees associated with membership.

» Hazing is demeaning. Don't participate!

3. Arrival on Campus

During the first week of term, thousands of new students flood university campuses. Everyone is interested in getting to know their new environment and in meeting lots of new people. Many will have arrived knowing few, if any, fellow students from their high school days. It is a time of great excitement and tension as everyone faces a period of self-reliance, challenge and opportunity. The combination of intense emotions that surrounds this experience can bring out a range of behaviours in new students. Some are better prepared for it than others. For you, it is a time to reflect on what you want out of that first week, to be prepared for the decisions you may have to make, and to remember what your values are as you make those decisions.

3.1   Frosh week

Frosh week provides an ideal opportunity for all new undergraduates to become active within the university community. You will be able to:

• Participate in various social and recreational events and learn more about the myriad of activities available at your university;

• Learn more about and meet the members of the various clubs and associations;

• Meet lots of new people in various programs;

• Participate in seminars and workshops to reinforce the life skills and the study skills you will need to succeed;

• Relax before your studies begin;

- Help with charity drives to raise money for various causes.
- Smile and say hi to everyone; most of the people you meet will be keen to make new friends. If you find this difficult, refer to Chapter 12.1. Think of this as an opportunity to talk to people who appear different from you. You will probably find they are interesting and lots of fun.

The Shinerama campaign raised $952,000 across Canada in 2003 to help fight cystic fibrosis. Students volunteered their time to shine shoes and wash cars.[23]

- Read all the handbooks distributed during Frosh week. They are full of good information specifically to help you. Keep them handy for future reference by filing them in your "University Info—Brochures" folder as suggested in Chapter 5.4.
- Be careful. There will be temptations to start off your term on the wrong foot by using street drugs and drinking alcohol excessively. You can have fun without doing either.
  » Many first- and second-year students have yet to reach the legal drinking age. Consequently, many campuses now have alcohol-free Frosh weeks;
  » Be sensible if you do drink, on or off campus;
  » Respect the choice of those who decide not to drink or use street drugs.
- Most "date rapes" occur during the first eight weeks of classes.[24]
  » Sexual intercourse that is forced, manipulated, or coerced by a partner, friend or acquaintance is a serious offence. It is date or acquaintance rape.[25] For most victims, it is traumatic. Date rape happens far too frequently.

Some sobering statistics on date rape:
- About 75 percent of men and at least 55 percent of women involved in acquaintance rape have been drinking or taking drugs before the attack.
- One out of every four women surveyed was a victim of rape or attempted rape.
- Eighty-four percent of those raped knew their attacker.[26]

23 Forty years of students fighting cystic fibrosis, Shinerama, downloaded from http://www.cysticfibrosis.ca/page.asp?id=33, March 2005.
24 Downloaded from http://carleton.ca/equity/gender/date_rape.htm on December 5, 2004.
25 Downloaded from http://carleton.ca/equity/gender/date_rape.htm on December 5, 2004.
26 Cited from Robin Warshaw, "I Never Called It Rape: The Ms. Report on Recognizing, Fighting, and Surviving Date and Acquaintance Rape," 1994 on http://carleton.ca/equity/gender/date_rape.htm downloaded December 5, 2004.

- Make good decisions to help you avoid the risk of either experiencing or committing date rape:
  - » Carefully consider what you want from a sexual relationship. Read through Chapter 13.13 and Appendix 4;
  - » Don't over indulge in alcohol; always pour your own drinks and keep them with you. Refer to Chapter 13.5 for more information on Roofies, also known as the date rape drug;
  - » Don't do street drugs;
  - » Party in groups; there is safety in numbers.
- Have fun but use Frosh week as an opportunity to get grounded for the term ahead.
  - » The first week of classes can be daunting. Don't make it worse by showing up hung over, sleep deprived, worried that you have screwed up a relationship, are pregnant, or have acquired a sexually transmitted infection.

3.2   Explore campus

Team up with someone else who is new and stroll around campus noting the location of Student Services, Health Services, the bookstore, student lounges, the cafeteria, and gathering spots for your social time.

Fifty-five percent of students report having used academic advisory services.[27]

- Stop by and see what services are offered.
- Say hello to the advisors. Advisors are there to assist you as you come up against challenges or just to answer simple questions.
  - » Advisors can become trusted friends through your years at university as you ponder the many choices ahead of you.

Some academic advisors are very efficient and "process your requirement." Others will take the time to connect with you personally. If you can, speak with a few different people to figure out whom you can work with best.

Paul, Carleton University, Arts '07

---

27   Survey of Undergraduate University Students: University of Winnipeg, 2002, downloaded from http://www.uwinnipeg.ca/index/cms-filesystem-action?file=pdfs/future/cusc.pdf on April 6, 2005.

Ask about campus safety programs, including the following:

- "Walk home" services which provide someone to escort you home in the evenings;
- Free engine boosts if your car battery dies;
- Theft prevention programs;
- Fire awareness programs.

Locate each of the classrooms and labs where your lectures will be held so you are not running around the halls lost and arriving late during the first week of classes.

Visit the library and sign up for an organized tour before your courses start.

- Ensure you are comfortable with the available technologies to assist your research;
- Familiarize yourself with the layout of the library and the location of books on your subject areas.

You are entitled to use the athletic facilities because a portion of your fees is contributing towards their support, so take advantage of them. Refer to Chapter 13.7.

- Register for at least one athletic program to keep your body and mind fit and healthy.
- Try something new.
- Seek advice from the staff at the athletic centre about available resources. There may be trainers to help you determine the best type of exercise for your body type and physical condition. There may be physical therapists to provide advice if you have suffered any previous sports injuries.

3.3   Getting organized

Now is a good time to check once again that the university's record of what you have registered for matches the courses you intended to select. Review the usual Web-based profile of your registration, or paper confirmations that the university may have sent to you. Make sure the course numbers and descriptions match your intentions.

- Many first year courses are offered in multiple sections. That is, the same course is offered more than once in the same term. Make special note of the section identifier, which is often a letter: i.e. Course 42.2504 Introductory Finance, Section H, or 42.2504H Introductory Finance.
- If you are lucky, the registration information, either Web- or paper-based, will indicate the course number, section identifier, course description, the name

of the professor, the time slot, and the classroom location. If not, there is probably a Web-based list of courses that links this information together. You need to link it all together to make sure you end up in the correct room on the first day of classes. Sometimes professors will post class lists outside their offices. If they do, check to see if your name is where it should be.

In my first year of University, my friends and I were attending the wrong accounting class for about three weeks. It was the same course, just a different professor. An academic advisor told us we were in the wrong section. We thought this was pretty funny. We went on the fourth week to our proper class, and had to write a quiz that day. The other section was behind a couple of chapters, so there were questions from chapters we had not even seen. The not-so-funny part was that all of us failed the quiz.

Tomo, University of Guelph, Business Administration '07

- Obtain your Student ID card, carry it everywhere and keep it safe. You will need it for exams, to enter the library and the gym, to use the Internet, to photocopy and maybe even to access certain buildings and use the elevators. It may even double as a debit card.
- Lockers are often rented on a first-come/first-served basis, so make this a priority if you plan on using the athletic centre regularly.

3.4   Textbooks

Purchase your textbooks as soon as possible. You may not have to wait for your course outline. Texts for each course may be listed on the university's Web site or in the bookstore. If you have your course outline, take it with you to the bookstore to help you find the required text(s).

- Believe it or not, there can be ordering or supply problems that lead to a shortage of textbooks in stock at the campus bookstore. Reordering can take a few weeks, which puts you behind in your reading and may put time pressures on the completion of your first assignment;
- Always check on-line booksellers to see if your texts are available. They may be less expensive there than at campus bookstores;
- Many university bookstores will buy and sell used texts. Getting to the bookstore early means you have a better chance of getting a second-hand text in good condition, which can save you a lot of money;

- Keep your receipts handy in the event you see an opportunity at a later date to buy the text second-hand. The receipt may enable you to return a text for full value. File receipts in your "Purchases" folder as suggested in Chapter 5.4.

- Check the edition number of your text and make sure it matches the edition specified in the course outline. Students often ask if the prior edition, which can often be found for half the cost of the new edition, is sufficient. Most of the time content improvements from edition to edition are marginal. However, if you decide to use the old edition, you are taking two basic risks:
  » Changes may be more than marginal;
  » Sequencing and numbering of pretty much everything in the book, chapters, sections, pages, problems, examples, equations, etc., are probably different in the new edition, which can make it more difficult to follow the professor's progression through the course. Most of the time, the cost savings aren't worth the risk. If you are less than an excellent student or are not superbly organized, buying an earlier edition to save a little money is definitely not worth the risk.

Before the first lecture, read each of the chapter headings and chapter summaries in your text. This will provide you with a frame of reference, which will make it easier to understand what the professor is doing in class.

- Course texts are often placed on reserve in the library. While this can be helpful sometimes (e.g., you are near the library, don't have your text with you, and need to refer to it), it is not a substitute for purchasing your own copy. The copies on reserve might be out on loan when you need them most.
- Required readings are sometimes placed on reserve in the library. Try to read these on or ahead of schedule, as competition for access to them can be intense later in the term as your less diligent classmates try to catch up. If the photocopying load is not too onerous, make your own copies so you can refer to them later in the term without another visit to the library, and without competing for access time with other students.

3.5   Chat with upper-year students

Talk to various students who have taken
your courses before and ask them what
their biggest challenges were, and plan
appropriately. This is what frosh week,
floor seniors in residence, and
upper-year students are there for.
Use them!

- Ask for tips on succeeding. Your
  fellow students may be willing to
  share their notes, assignments and
  tests with you, but be sure to use
  such sources only as support for
  your studying, and not for
  plagiarism.
- Experienced students can be extremely helpful in advising who the good
  professors are and which elective courses to take or avoid.
- Be bold. Talk to upper year students who may be hanging out in the halls of
  the department related to the course in which you are interested. Most
  students enjoy sharing their experiences.

3.6   Consider a non-credit course

If your math, communication or writing skills are weak,
consider taking a non-credit course or auditing a course
to improve your skills. Student Services can refer you or
provide you with the relevant information.

> **Eighty-three**
> percent of students
> using study skills/
> learning support
> services report being
> satisfied with their
> experience.[28]

- If you expect your program will involve a large
  amount of reading, or if you are a slow reader,
  consider taking a course that will improve your
  reading speed and effectiveness.
- Although you may have passed the prerequisite
  courses, be realistic about whether you need to enhance your skills. For
  example, if you barely passed calculus in high school but will use it in

---

28   Survey of Undergraduate University Students: University of Winnipeg, 2002, downloaded from
      http://www.uwinnipeg.ca/index/cms-filesystem-action?file=pdfs/future/cusc.pdf on April 6, 2005.

upcoming science or engineering courses, then consider a refresher course, or a self-study program, to enhance your understanding. This will make your university courses much more manageable.

3.7   Special needs

If you are a person with a learning disability or a physical disability, ask Student Services for a referral to the appropriate support group.

- Ask about and take advantage of the help that is available to you.
- As we indicated in Chapter 2.3, some medical conditions entitle you to specific accommodations at university, such as extra time to write exams, a room to yourself to write exams, or specially adapted technological support. These accommodations are there for you because the university cares about your success, wants you to have appropriate support, and wants you to use what is available.

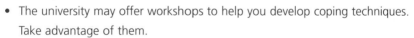
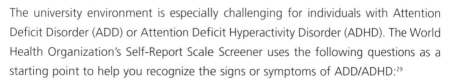

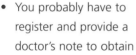

- You probably have to register and provide a doctor's note to obtain the accomodations referred to above. Use the one we suggested you obtain in Chapter 2.3.
- The university may offer workshops to help you develop coping techniques. Take advantage of them.

The university environment is especially challenging for individuals with Attention Deficit Disorder (ADD) or Attention Deficit Hyperactivity Disorder (ADHD). The World Health Organization's Self-Report Scale Screener uses the following questions as a starting point to help you recognize the signs or symptoms of ADD/ADHD:[29]

» How often do you have trouble wrapping up the final details of a project once the challenging parts have been done?

---

29   Adult Self-Report Scale (ASRS - V1.1) Screener from WHO Composite International Diagnostic Interview, © World Health Organization.

- » How often do you have difficulty getting things in order when you have to do a task that requires organization?
- » How often do you have problems remembering appointments or obligations?
- » When you have a task that requires a lot of thought, how often do you avoid or delay getting started?
- » How often do you fidget or squirm with your hands or feet when you have to sit down for a long time?
- » How often do you feel overly active and compelled to do things, as if you were driven by a motor?[30]

- A tendency to engage in the behaviours addressed in the questions is indicative of ADD/ADHD.
- Some individuals who exhibit signs of ADD/ADHD have been diagnosed with the disorder, while others have not, possibly out of a desire to avoid labelling a child with ADD/ADHD within the elementary and high school systems. Individuals with ADD/ADHD, who are likely to engage in the behaviours outlined in the questions, are going to find university quite difficult. Succeeding in high school is not necessarily an indication that all is well, as an individual's support system, the workload, and the complexity of the work can be much different in university. If you exhibit signs of ADD/ADHD, let your doctor know. Diagnosis can lead to treatment and an awareness of coping skills that can make a significant difference in the quality of your life at university.
- If you are a person with ADD/ADHD, you can take some steps to help you enjoy your time at university:
  - » First, accept your situation and realize that you will have more challenges than most other students. Identify your main difficulties and be honest about them when evaluating opportunities and when speaking to counsellors;
  - » You need to make the choice to succeed. Support systems will do you no good unless you have the inner drive to do well despite the hurdles you deal with on a daily basis;
  - » Ask your doctor about recent developments in medication. However, even with medication, it is still easy to become distracted from your priorities, so you may have to use other strategies as well;
  - » Depending on the magnitude of your challenges, consider starting off with a lighter course load until you establish a new routine;

---

30   These questions do not replace consultation with your physician, as an accurate diagnosis can only be made through a clinical evaluation. Regardless of how you may have answered the foregoing questions, consult your doctor if you have concerns about a diagnosis of ADD/ADHD.

» Ask Student Services if they know of any workshops that might help you develop additional coping skills;

» Sign up for a time management and organizational course through Student Services. Use our *University Matters Student Planner* and read Chapter 5;

» Ask about the possibility of an upper-year student or advisor being assigned to you to act as a mentor and help keep you directed. Meeting with someone once a week will help keep you on track, even if it's only fifteen minutes for coffee on Friday afternoons;

» Try to figure out when and how you learn best so you can select courses that are taught in a style that works for you, are scheduled in suitable time slots, and address material you find interesting. Pick a quiet place to study, free from distractions. Refer to Chapter 6;

» A diagnosis of ADD or ADHD may entitle you to accommodations like those we mentioned above, and in Chapter 2.3.

I really appreciate the support structure that Carleton has in place to help me. I have ADHD and take medication, but still struggle on a daily basis with the challenges of ADHD. I was diagnosed when I was seven; you'd think I'd have it figured out by now! I have attended wrong class sections, forgotten my student ID card when going to exams, often forget to take my medication, leave important books in my room, continue to give in assignments late due to poor planning...you name it. I screw up daily! I really don't want to and am always looking for better coping skills. I have great TAs and advisors available to help me. I won't graduate with an A average, but I am learning so many interesting things, meeting tons of fun people, having the time of my life, and finally realizing it is my choice to succeed. My advice? Don't be afraid to seek help. There's a great support structure that has been designed to help students who need extra support, so use it!

Paul, Carleton University, Sociology and Human Rights '07

3.8   Extracurricular activities

Extracurricular activities can be very rewarding and increase your sense of personal fulfillment and belonging in your new community. They can also enhance your resume and make you more attractive to potential employers because they:

» Build your leadership skills;

» Improve your problem-solving ability;

» Develop your creativity;

» Demonstrate initiative;

» Show that you have the ability to manage your time to achieve balance in your life.

It's really important to get involved and not be intimidated by upper-year students who are running the clubs and organizations. It's so awesome to interact regularly with upper years since they can offer tons of good tips.

Zoe, Queen's University, ArtSci '08

- Many employers are moving towards competency-based hiring, making this aspect of university life much more important for long-term success. They want to hire people who have been involved in the world around them, and who are attuned to the socio-economic and political challenges of today.
- Sadly some prospective employers still screen only by marks in the initial recruiting rounds. Ask your professors about the importance of marks versus work experience in your field.
- Extracurricular commitments can consume a lot of your time and negatively affect your academic performance. It is easy to end up devoting more time and energy to running for the student government than to your courses. There are a few factors to consider before committing, such as:
    » The amount of time that is involved;
    » When your time will be needed;
    » How organized you are and how well you manage your time. If it's a struggle, take on only a small commitment;
    » The extent to which the academic demands on you will increase as the term progresses.
- Evaluate whether the extracurricular activities you are considering meet your personal goals. Refer to Chapter 1.2 and the Personal Goals Worksheet in your *University Matters Student Planner* or downloadable at www.universitymatters.ca. Choose activities that allow you to express yourself. Find your outlet, whether it is in the arts, sports or student government.

Forty-three percent of students participate in community-service or volunteer activities either on or off campus.[31]

---

31   Survey of Undergraduate University Students: University of Winnipeg, 2002, downloaded from
     http://www.uwinnipeg.ca/index/cms-filesystem-action?file=pdfs/future/cusc.pdf on April 6, 2005.

- Working in a student association, or in student government, can be very empowering. You may find out that you are capable of more than you had imagined, and that you can initiate change in the world.
- If you plan to apply to Medical School or to a Faculty of Education, a solid record of volunteering in your chosen field will be a significant asset.
- Consider allocating some of your time to volunteer activities.
- Most campuses maintain a database of volunteer opportunities within the local community. If not, search the town or city Web site for contact information for the local Volunteer Bureau.
- Besides the numerous resume-enhancing skills you can acquire, you will develop immense satisfaction from helping others and furthering causes you believe in.
- Volunteering may be your passion or a simple commitment to devote one hour a week to helping others. Be firm with yourself and the organization about your available time. Try not to overcommit because you could become overwhelmed and quit altogether.
- Contact the local library or literacy group and offer to read with a child or adult for one hour each week. Although this is a fairly small time commitment, you can make an incredible difference to someone's life. In Canada, 42 percent of adults aged 16 to 65 cannot meet most everyday reading requirements.[32] Their children suffer accordingly.
- Contact the local hospital and offer to visit patients who might not have family nearby.
- Support the Canadian Landmine Foundation by participating in their fundraising event, the Night of a Thousand Dinners. This year the organizers are encouraging young people to inspire family-based dinners. Encourage your parents to host a dinner for friends, family and neighbours. Tell them that you are personally going to make a commitment to the event. If you are living in your own house or apartment, host a dinner or a social event. There are all sorts of things you can do:
  » Help put together the guest list;

---

32   Statistics Canada, *Adult Literacy and Life Skills Survey*, May 11, 2005.

- » Design a special invitation—be creative;
- » Help select the menu (go to www.1000dinners.com or search the net for recipes from mine-affected countries);
- » Help prepare the meal;
- » Help to serve the meal;
- » Help clean up;
- » Do a short presentation about landmines for the guests (see www.canadianlandmine.org for ideas).

SHOW THE WORLD THAT YOU CARE!

I started volunteering while I was in high school: reading to children, organizing coffeehouses for battered women's shelters, participating in many CNIB and Canadian Cancer Society fundraising campaigns. In 2000, when I heard a presentation from a Columbian landmine survivor, I stepped up my efforts. I volunteered for Mines Action Canada and the Youth Mine Action Ambassador Program, played a central role in organizing Canadian Landmine Awareness Week for four consecutive years, and, in November 2004, had the chance to travel to Kenya to attend the Nairobi Summit on a Mine-Free World as a youth delegate. This was the review conference on the Mine Ban Treaty, and united all people involved in the campaign to ban landmines.

I have met landmine survivors and activists from all over the world through the International Campaign to Ban Landmines (ICBL): the most phenomenal and inspiring people ever! I am going to spend my third year of university in Peru through Canada World Youth, a cultural exchange program between Canada and developing countries, and hope to continue volunteering for the International Campaign to Ban Landmines and other NGOs upon my return. I am looking forward to a career in international development, focusing on human rights and education.

There is nothing quite like volunteering. Giving up your time and energy to help other people is more rewarding than most people realize. The skills that I have developed through my volunteer work, not only with the ICBL, but with other organizations as well, would have been impossible for me to learn any other way. I have been given the opportunity to travel, to meet incredible people, and to actually make a small difference in the way that the world works. Educating people is the first step to improving the situation in which many people live, and volunteering has made me realize that I can do that while educating myself at the same time. There are a few things that any student can organize to raise awareness and support for causes and organizations. Benefit concerts, like the one my friends and I organized that raised $2,500 for Tsunami relief, or dinners, like the Night of a Thousand Dinners (www.1000dinners.com), where people host dinners to raise money to clear landmines, are really effective events.

Getting involved in these sorts of things is the best thing I have ever done. The direction of my life has changed, and I learn more about others and myself every time I participate in a volunteer event. All you have to do is look around, and you will find someone or something that needs your help, and where you really can make a difference.

Elodie, University of Ottawa,
International Development and Globalization '08

3.9   Part-time employment

Ideally it would be nice to avoid having a part-time job during the school year.

- Academic studies are a full-time job. However, financial realities may demand that you juggle a part-time job with your studies. Many students do. Some students who are not under financial pressure take on a part-time job related to their future career to gain work experience and enhance their resume.

52% Fifty-two percent of full-time undergraduate students in Canadian universities spend an average of 18 hours a week at work, and 60 percent of them report that their jobs have at least some negative impact on their academic performance.

10% Ten percent of those not working are looking for a job.

40% About 40 percent of first-year students report having a job, while 60 percent of fourth-year students report having employment.[33]

- Before you commit to a job, take into consideration the workload of your program. Some degree programs are more demanding than others. Start off

---

33   Survey of Undergraduate University Students: University of Winnipeg, 2002, downloaded from http://www.uwinnipeg.ca/index/cms-filesystem-action?file=pdfs/future/cusc.pdf on April 6, 2005.

with a commitment of about ten hours per week. As the term progresses you will see whether you can handle any additional hours.

Advise your employer that you are a student with tuition and education deductions and fill out the necessary forms so that income tax is not withheld from your earnings.

- Time management is the key to success for students who are balancing school work and a part-time job. Use your *University Matters Student Planner* to manage your commitments as suggested in Chapter 5.
- You may find that having a part-time job is beneficial in that it forces you to manage your time and avoid procrastination.
- You will probably have to sacrifice a chunk of your social time if you have a part-time job during the school year.
- On-campus jobs are sometimes reserved for students in financial need.
- Try to find a job that allows you to read in your spare time, such as one at a self-serve gas station.
- If you are committed to your studies and create a strong rapport with your professors, you may be considered for a teaching assistant position.
- Babysitting is flexible, and late evening jobs may provide you with a few hours to study. Post signs in the local grocery stores indicating your availability and that you can provide references.

My biggest lesson over the past four years comes not from school itself, but from having a job (and at times, two jobs) during school. I didn't have to do this, but because of it I have learned to be very organized and financially aware. Having a job during school forced me to plan my days, get down to work when I had the time—and most importantly, I learned the value of a dollar! On that note, I think it is important to realize that it is possible to have a part-time job and be in school. The amount of time students actually spend reading, writing and studying is definitely much less than the time they spend sleeping, socializing and going out. Setting aside fifteen hours a week for a job is workable, especially in an Arts program! For engineers this is probably not going to work.

Jenn, Carleton University,

Arts '05 Honours Political Science and Classics/Religion

---

4. The First Few Weeks of Classes

The first few weeks of classes are an opportunity for you to enjoy the results of all the preparation you have undertaken so far. All that you anticipated is now a reality. It will be exciting and very busy. There are some administrative things you need to know to ensure you get the classes you want, and some strategies for setting you up on a solid platform for the term ahead. We discuss them in this chapter.

4.1   Full classes

Pleading with the professor to get into a full class because "it fits into your schedule" generally won't get you in. On the other hand, if you have a truly compelling reason for having registered late, need the class as a prerequisite, or are genuinely keen on the course content but did not get in, approach the professor in person and explain your case. While full classes are a problem for students and professors alike, you are much more likely to enlist the professor's support if you have good academic reasons for your request.

- Have all the necessary paperwork on hand to make it easy for the professor to approve your request.
  - » Generally you will need a course add/drop form. Fill out everything on the form that you can before presenting yourself to the professor. Obviously, presenting the professor with a blank form to complete seriously undermines your argument that you are keen to take the course.
- If you have trouble getting an appointment to see the professor, attend the first few classes, sit near the front, and participate.
  - » Show your enthusiasm and commitment in person;
  - » Your e-mail request won't stand out versus the others the professor is probably receiving;
  - » If someone drops out, you can offer to take his or her place. Your presence will help support your request.

4.2   Course outlines

In order to be successful you must understand what is expected of you. In short, course outlines spell this out.

- Read the course outline carefully to understand the learning objectives and how marks will be allocated. This gives you important context for all that follows in the course.

- Highlight important information and keep the outline in your course binder. Refer to it each week. It is your road map.
  - » It tells you where you have been, where you are now, and where you are going;
  - » It tells you what to do, and for key items, when to do them;
  - » It tells you the allocation of marks to tasks, and in some cases, the principles underlying the awarding of marks;
  - » Of all the questions asked by students at a professor's door, probably 90 percent are answered in the course outline. Imagine how bad you look asking your professor for information that is written on the course outline that he or she gave you and that you should have in your binder.
- Write an e-mail to your professor if you notice that a test or exam has been scheduled on a religious observance date. If you let him or her know early enough, the date may be changed. Otherwise, an accommodation may be made for you to write on an alternate date. Check your university's Web site and undergraduate calendar for full information on religious accommodations.

4.3 Course changes

- If you don't like a professor's style, try to switch sections.
- If the course content is different from what you expected, drop the course and register in one you like better.
- If you are having trouble deciding which course or section to take, find some classes that aren't full yet and attend a few lectures to see if you like the subject matter and the professor's approach. This makes for a very full schedule in the first few weeks, but it is well worth the extra effort.
- Consult an academic advisor before dropping a prerequisite for your program. Prerequisite structures can be complex webs, and missing out on one early on may affect your ability to register for a full load of courses in the future. This is an area where academic advisors often have a lot of expertise, and can be very helpful.

- Ensure you follow the correct procedures to withdraw from a course or you may have a failure recorded on your transcript. Once you are registered in a course, the only options are to be awarded a mark or to withdraw. If you don't withdraw you will be given a "fail" on your transcript, even though you never showed up for a single lecture.
- Most employers recruiting at the university will ask you to include your transcript with your resume when applying for a job. You don't want to have to show them one with a failure on it. They have no way of knowing whether you did miserably in the course and failed, or simply forgot to withdraw.
- Act early when withdrawing from a course to maximize any available fee refunds.
- Withdrawing from a course could change your status from full-time to part-time. This status has nothing to do with how much time you spend on your university studies and is determined only by the number of courses you are taking. There could be implications:
  - » Various bursaries, scholarships, student loan arrangements, residence eligibility and other such things may require full-time enrolment and may be withdrawn if you do not meet this requirement. For example, in some cases, a student bus pass is available only to full-time students;
  - » Income tax savings for you or your parents will change, as the education deduction will be reduced from $400 per month to $120 per month. Refer to Chapter 15.6 for more details.

4.4   Getting to know your classmates

- Say hello to classmates. Refer to Chapter 12.1 if you find it difficult to initiate conversation.
- Get acquainted with classmates early so you can figure out which individuals you want to work with in study groups or for group assignments. Refer to Chapter 9.1.

- Team up with two classmates, exchange contact information and agree to provide notes to each other if one of you is sick and misses a class.
- Reviewing two sets of notes will clarify the key points, and one classmate might explain some points better than the other.
- Don't abuse this courtesy. Your classmates will quickly become resentful if they perceive they are being used as your note takers.

4.5   Getting used to your new environment

Don't underestimate the stresses associated with a new place, new people and new routines. Give yourself some time to adjust.

- Many students who were popular in high school feel a sense of loss and confusion when they enter a new environment where they feel insignificant initially. Give yourself a chance to get settled. Smile at everyone. Refer to Chapter 12.1.
- The sooner you get to know other students and develop a sense of belonging in your new community, the sooner you will be able to focus on enjoying life as a university student.
- Check out what you can do in the local community, such as attending poetry readings or listening to local bands.
- Attend meetings and talks on campus to broaden your thinking.
- Go to a varsity football, hockey or basketball game with a couple of other newcomers. A varsity sporting event on campus can be lots of fun!

If you are living away from home, you will probably feel homesick. For some the feeling is minor. For others it can be a larger issue. Minor feelings of homesickness arise because the familiar has been replaced with the unknown, which causes most people some level of anxiety. You have probably left behind some very special people and you may miss them more than you anticipated. You may also feel you have fewer friends than you are used to, which can lead to feelings of loneliness and inadequacy. This can be unsettling if you usually feel confident and in charge of your life.

- Many other students will be feeling the same way you do. Reach out to them, smile, and share your concerns and anxieties.
- If you find you are having difficulty with homesickness, go to Health Services to discuss how you feel. They are there to help you.
- Explore the local community to get a sense of your new environment. Invite another newcomer to join you. Go to the local tourist office so you can get a good sense of what's in town.
- Get involved in campus activities as soon as you have a sense of your time commitments for academics.
- Remember that sleep deprivation, hangovers, and insufficient nutrition will magnify the things that cause you to worry. Give yourself the best shot at adjusting to your new environment by looking after your health.
- Keep in touch with family and friends back home, but make sure you direct your energy towards saying hello to someone new every day.
- Give yourself some time to settle in. Resist the urge to go home every other weekend. Pick a date, like Thanksgiving, and look forward to seeing your friends and family then. Most students have very positive experiences if they give themselves the time to settle in and make new friends. New friends don't replace old friends; they are additional friends.

90% Ninety percent of students have positive impressions of their universities in terms of treating students fairly.

86% Eighty-six percent of students feel they have had an intellectually stimulating experience at university.

70% Seventy percent feel they are a part of their university.[34]

---

34   Survey of Undergraduate University Students: University of Winnipeg, 2002, downloaded from
     http://www.uwinnipeg.ca/index/cms-filesystem-action?file=pdfs/future/cusc.pdf on April 6, 2005.

NOTES

Staying Organized

SECTION TWO

• • •

Staying Organized

Pretty much all of university life is a race against time. There will be many more interesting and exciting opportunities than you can possibly take advantage of. You will find an abundance of opportunity in almost every aspect of your university life: socially, academically, athletically and artistically. So how do you get the most out of your experience at university while still holding it all together? There are no quick fixes that will work for everyone, but following some of the suggestions in this section will certainly help.

Biggest Challenges

- Getting into the daily habit of writing everything down
- Sticking to your schedule
- Learning how to say no

5. Tempus Fugit: Time Flies

Time is the most valuable and vulnerable aspect of university life. Spend it as if you have too little of it. Allocate it as if it were a precious commodity. It is.

Much of this chapter is devoted to setting up your life's commitments in your *University Matters Student Planner*, and then living by it. To some, this can seem lacking in flexibility and spontaneity. But it is actually the opposite. If you manage your time, you are in charge of your life, which gives you the flexibility to respond to opportunities as they arise. If you don't manage your time, there is little that stands between you and the uncomfortable crunch of multiple deadlines—too much to do, too little time to do it. The argument that you are a free spirit and don't need to plan your time is seriously flawed. It is only a matter of time until events conspire to rob you of your illusion of freedom.

Lost, yesterday, somewhere between sunrise and sunset, two golden hours, each set with sixty diamond minutes. No reward is offered, for they are gone forever.

Horace Mann

5.1 Managing your time

Use the *University Matters Student Planner* to manage your many commitments. You can order a copy from www.universitymatters.ca. Using the *University Matters Student Planner* will help you to:

- Plan for success through to the end of the school year;
- Stick to your priorities;
- Meet your deadlines;
- Remember important dates;
- Pay your bills on time;
- Keep your appointments;
- Achieve your goals;
- Identify a convergence of commitments (oh no!), prompting you to reschedule work so you can...
- *Plan for success through to the end of the school year!*

The freedom in university is exhilarating. However, the lack of boundaries means you can get off track easily. Use your *University Matters Student Planner*, and its various worksheets and checklists, to enjoy your freedom while managing your commitments.

If you haven't had to do much planning so far in your life, your first attempt can be stressful. You will find it a bit daunting to take all the things you might do, need to do, should do or must do, and convert it all from the hodgepodge in your mind, or the accumulated scraps of paper in your pockets, to the seemingly rigid structure of a personal calendar. The prospect of doing this is stressful, which motivates many to accept the status quo, and muddle along forever. But you *can* do better, and you will *need* to do better!

• Reality check: as you get busier and busier at university, the number of things you have to keep track of will grow and grow. At the same time, the amount of mental capacity available to juggle your schedule in your head will shrink and shrink. This happens because you will be composing your next paper in your head as you walk around campus, instead of pondering your schedule. Eventually, a cataclysmic conflict between what you need to keep track of and what you are able to keep track of will occur. This is called total chaos. Although it manifests itself in various ways, you will identify it right away. Here are some examples:

» Showing up to class on the day of the mid-term, thinking the mid-term is actually next week;

» That sinking feeling that arises when everyone except you arrives at class with a completed assignment in hand and plunks it down on the prof's desk; or, even worse,

» Realizing partway through a good game of pool at about 10 p.m. that you had a date with someone you care about at 9 p.m.

• The cure is to assign the task of keeping track of everything in your life to your *University Matters Student Planner*. Again, this may be stressful at first, but is not nearly as stressful as a cataclysmic attack of chaos, or your roommate accidentally washing your jeans with half a pound of paper scraps of "To Do" notes hidden in the pockets.

• Give it a try! Commit to spending 5 to 10 minutes at the same time every day to allocate your time and review your schedule.

» Some people do this in the evening before bed; others prefer first thing in the morning;

» The time spent planning will be reduced as it eventually becomes second nature;

» When you take a few quiet moments to have a cup of coffee, scan your schedule, and regroup; the experience can actually be fun and empowering.

• Planning relieves stress and allows you to enjoy your downtime guilt-free. Being able to see your obligations for the weeks ahead written down in your *University Matters Student Planner* is very helpful.

» If your time in the days ahead is mapped out, a glance at your planner will tell you how tight your time is, or alternatively, how much slack time you have;

» You will feel better when you have all your tasks blocked out in your planner, knowing that you are in control of the time ahead and can get everything done;

» You will have many demands on your time and you may have to reduce time allocated to low-priority tasks during busy weeks. Use your planner to help make these decisions;

» Without an organized approach it is easy to forget tasks that need to be done and to miss deadlines. With an organized approach, you won't need to worry about them;

» Without an organized approach there is a tendency to address tasks in order of their difficulty; that is, do the easy tasks first and defer the difficult ones. This gives you the illusion of progress, but it won't get you where you want to go;

» Procrastinating and wasting time are easy to do. Time gets away from you quickly, and often studying is what suffers most. Procrastination will have a direct effect on your future available time. Avoid this common and costly tendency.

• If you think you are "too busy to be organized," think again!

Carpe Diem: Seize the Day

5.2   Identify the many demands on your time

When you start using your *University Matters Student Planner,* consider the following time demands, as well as those specific to you:

Daily Academic

- Classes
- Tutorials
- Workshops and labs
- Group meetings
- Midterm tests and final exams
- Thinking time

- Scheduled chapters and other reading
- Research
- Assignments
- Projects
- Presentations
- Practice tests

Daily Life

- Planning your day
- Personal hygiene
- Preparing and eating nutritious meals
- Exercise and team sports
- Sleep
- Commuting back and forth

- Keeping your living space clean and tidy
- Medical, dental and other personal appointments
- Birthdays and other important dates
- Downtime

Weekly Life

- Part-time job
- Cleaning your living space
- Grocery shopping
- Dates and other social commitments

- Hobbies and extracurricular activities
- Volunteer work
- Expected trips home
- Laundry

Philosophy Lesson[35]

A philosophy professor stood before his class and had some items in front of him. When the class began, wordlessly he picked up a very large and empty mayonnaise jar and proceeded to fill it with rocks, rocks about 2" (5 cms) in diameter. He then asked the students if the jar was full. They agreed that it was. So the professor then picked up a box of pebbles, and poured them into the jar. He shook the jar lightly. The pebbles of course rolled into the open areas between the rocks. He then asked the students again if the jar was full. They agreed it was.

The professor picked up a box of sand and poured it into the jar. Of course the sand filled up everything else. He then asked once more if the jar was full. The students responded unanimously yes.

The professor then produced two cans of beer from under the table and proceeded to pour their entire contents into the jar, effectively filling the empty space between the sand. The students laughed.

"Now," said the professor, as the laughter subsided, "I want you to recognize that this jar represents your life.

"The rocks are the important things—your family, your partner, your health, your children—things that if everything else was lost and only they remained, your life would still be full.

"The pebbles are the other things that matter like your job, your house, your car.

"The sand is everything else. The small stuff."

"If you put the sand in the jar first," he continued, "there is no room for the pebbles or the rocks. The same goes for your life. If you spend all your time and energy on the small stuff, you will never have room for the things that are important to you. Pay attention to the things that are critical to your happiness. Play with your children. Take time to get medical checkups. Take your partner out dancing. There will always be time to go to work, clean the house, give a dinner party and fix the disposal. Take care of the rocks first— the things that really matter. Set your priorities. The rest is just sand."

One of the students raised her hand and inquired what the beer represented. The professor smiled. "I'm glad you asked. It just goes to show you that no matter how full your life may seem, there's always room for a couple of beers."

5.3   Using your *University Matters Student Planner*

Always carry your *University Matters Student Planner* with you.

For many, having a visual representation of the tasks to come, and the time allotted to achieve them, is incredibly useful.

The following suggestions will keep you super-organized. If they seem overwhelming, start with a few of them. Adopt additional suggestions as you become more comfortable with using your *University Matters Student Planner.* For example, if you are good at managing your expenses, you may not need to track your expenditures right away.

You can have fun with this: use markers, highlighters, different coloured ink, stickers or a plain old pencil. The key is to develop a system that works well for you.

Before the term starts:
- Identify as many dates that are important to you as possible and write them into your *University Matters Student Planner.* Some examples include:
  » Last day for registering in a course;
  » Last day to withdraw from a course with a refund of fees;
  » Last date to withdraw from a course without academic penalty;
  » Reading week;
  » First day of classes;
  » Last day of classes;
  » Start and end of exam periods;
  » Birthdays.
- Record in your *University Matters Student Planner* the times of classes, labs, workshops and tutorials for the term ahead. This is a laborious task but worth doing so that you do not mistakenly make another commitment during class time.

During your first week of classes:
- Refer to each of your course outlines and identify the key tasks that need to be completed for each course.
- Make entries in your *University Matters Student Planner* for all due dates assigned to papers, assignments, projects, lab reports or tests.
  » Mark down the due date;

SEPTEMBER, 2005				
12 • Monday	**13 • Tuesday**	**14 • Wednesday**	**15 • Thursday**	**16 • Friday**
8 AM	8 AM	8 AM	8 AM	8 AM
9	9 *Intro to Symbolic Logic PASS-00*	9 *Political Thought TA Group*	9 *Introduction to Symbolic Logic PASS-00*	9 *History of Political Thought*
10	10	10	10	10
11	11	11 *History of Political Thought PASS-00*	11	11 *History of War in Europe*
12 Noon	12 Noon	12 Noon	12 Noon	12 Noon
1	1	1 *History of War in Europe CLASS*	1	1
2	2	2	2	2
3 *Intro to Political Science PASS-00*	3	3 *Introduction to Political Science*	3 *Seminar Interpretation of Religion CLASS*	3
4	4	4	4	4
5 *Political Science CLASS*	5	5	5	5
6	6	6	6	6
7	7	7	7	7
8	8	8	8	8
9	9	9	9	9
10	10	10	10	10
11	11	11	11	11
12 Midnight	12 Midnight	12 Midnight	12 Midnight	12 Midnight

» Make a reminder entry two weeks prior to the due date of an assignment indicating that the due date is coming up and that you now need to block out the time to address the task at hand;

» Submission dates may not be established in your course outline, but your professor should be able to give you a rough idea of when the work will be due. Ask in the first class. When they are announced, enter them in your *University Matters Student Planner* right away.

• Note the office hours for each of your professors and teaching assistants on the Professors' Contact Details Worksheet in your *University Matters Student Planner.* Take advantage of this time; it has been set aside for you.

• If you have a scheduling conflict for tutorials, an assignment or a test, approach the professor early on with an explanation and ask for accommodation.

Use your *University Matters Student Planner* on a daily basis.

• Keep track of everything you have to get done and prioritize the importance of each task as suggested in the Philosophy Lesson (see page 82). If there are a lot of items, allocate them into groups such as:

» Must do this week (the rocks);

» Want to do this week (the pebbles);

» Nice to do this week (the sand).

• Allocate time in your schedule first to the "Must Do" items to ensure they get done.

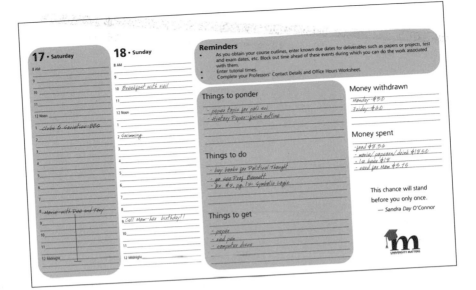

- If you make a new personal commitment, establish a date for acting on it, and block out in your *University Matters Student Planner* the time you will need for it.
- Record academic commitment due dates as soon as each new assignment is announced.
- For each due date, block off the time that will be required to do the associated work, working backwards from the due date. By doing this you will quickly see if your schedule is full in the days before the due date, and you can compensate by doing the work earlier.
- Break large tasks or longer assignments into manageable pieces and estimate how many hours you need to set aside to complete each piece of the assignment. Block these out in your *University Matters Student Planner*. For example:
  » Research the topic—estimated time: four hours;
  » Prepare outline of paper—estimated time: two hours;
  » Write sections one, two and three—estimated time: two, three and three hours for a total of eight hours;
  » Review complete paper—estimated time: two hours.
- Students often underestimate how much time is needed for each study task. A benefit of writing down your planned time allocations for tasks is that you will be able to observe how accurate your estimates were. The more you estimate and, later, compare to the actual time spent, the more accurate your estimates will become.

- Additionally, block off three hours of non-specific study time each week in case you underestimate time required for certain tasks and for unforeseen eventualities. If you do not need to use the three hours for studying, you will have extra downtime available to socialize, or head for the gym.

It's great not to have the pressure of submitting an assignment every day as in high school. There is more incentive to do well because assignments are worth a decent portion of your final mark, rather than just five percent. However, if you don't manage your time properly you end up in trouble. Whenever I get a few assignments that are all due around the same time, I know that I'll be faced with time-management challenges—not one of my strengths! I have a real tendency to underestimate the volume of work that goes into writing a great paper; funny considering I've written about 20 papers up to this point. Nevertheless, it seems that I consistently leave the minimum time required to write a paper that I know I could have done better on had I given myself more time. This tends to happen a lot more frequently when the due dates of assignments are clustered together. When this happens it is extremely important for me to spread out my workload because I know that I can't work non-stop for five to six days in an attempt to complete two or three papers in that time period. Often when I try that method, not only does the quality of work diminish but also, for the few days that I've left myself to cram, I skip classes and keeping up with my readings suffers. My advice? Make realistic timelines, aiming to get papers done at certain times, and know your limits when it comes to sitting down and writing because it's common to overestimate the amount of work you can do in a short period of time. It's important to consider the time it takes to research your topic, write your paper, and edit it, as well as the fact that all of this must be structured around current classes, and assigned readings. I'm still working on perfecting this!

Paul, Carleton University, Arts '07

- Consider whether any of your commitments can be done while multi-tasking, such as when doing your laundry, going for a walk or commuting.
- Try using a coloured pencil to cross off completed items so you have a visual sense of accomplishment. Checking off completed items is extremely satisfying, especially when you are working on a large project.

- At the end of the day, ensure any uncompleted tasks are moved forward to an available time slot that is far enough in advance of the due date to leave adequate time for completion.
- If you "fall off the wagon" because you are not used to writing your commitments down and sticking to a schedule, don't hesitate to start afresh!
- Your *University Matters Student Planner* is a useful tool that is meant to work for you. Once you get used to the benefits of planning, you will love it!
- Succumbing to spontaneity is OK some of the time, as long as there are some empty time slots in the days ahead. By writing everything down in your planner and being able to see the combination of committed and empty time slots ahead of you, you will feel more comfortable with occasionally deviating from your schedule.

> - If you are using the bus or train, use this time for reading or studying key notes.
> - If you are driving, walking or riding a bike, use this time to think through your approach to upcoming assignments.
> - Practice deep breathing and use commuting time to relax

- Use the "Things to Do" lists in your *University Matters Student Planner* to keep track of items without a specific due date. For example, you may have promised to burn a CD for a friend. Allocate tasks to available time slots if you prefer.
- Cross each item off the list when completed.
- Each Sunday evening or Monday morning, move any uncompleted items forward to the next week.

- Update the "Things to Get" list in your *University Matters Student Planner* as things pop into your mind.
- Use the "Things to Ponder" list in your *University Matters Student Planner* to keep track of things you need to think about. Consult the list when you have a bit of free time, over coffee, for example, or while commuting, to make good use of what is otherwise downtime. For example:
  - » What shall I get Mom for her birthday?
  - » Which topic shall I pick for my term paper?
- Keep track of where your money is going by jotting down what you buy together with the related cost.

Use the worksheets and checklists in your *University Matters Student Planner* to keep yourself organized. These documents can also be downloaded from www.universitymatters.ca.

- Record each professor's and teaching assistant's office hours and contact information on the Professors' Contact Details Worksheet.
- Add items to your Supply Top-Up Checklist and use it to shop effectively and efficiently, perhaps on a visit back home.
- Record your successes as they occur. When you are job hunting you will need to provide examples to future employers.
  - » Record things you do well;
  - » Note any difficulties you overcame. Prospective employers will sometimes ask about this. Being able to discuss a difficulty you faced and how you overcame it will impress them;
  - » Record your personal achievements;
  - » From time to time, use these notes to update the Resume Builder Worksheet.
- Review your personal goals, record them on the Personal Goals Worksheet in your *University Matters Student Planner,* and stay on track. When you meet your goals, reward yourself. If you study efficiently and manage your time, you will be able to enjoy something fun without feeling guilty that you are not studying.

You will manage your time better if you learn to say no when your schedule is full. This might mean declining a social invitation that you would really like to accept, or declining to help someone, which can be difficult. Explain that your time is fully blocked out and, if you can, suggest an alternate date that works better for you.

5.4   Set up filing systems

Managing your paperwork and computer files is much like managing your "To Do" list. If you keep track of papers and files as you go along, it will become a habit that hardly takes any time. If you don't, then the resulting chaos will waste hours of your time and increase your stress level. Staying organized as you go along will eliminate the stress and wasted time associated with trying to find an article or document that you "know you have somewhere."

- Keep a binder for each course and keep all relevant course material in that binder. You may prefer an expandable folder in which you keep manila folders for notes, readings and assignments. Or you can use a three-ring binder and section dividers to stay organized.
- Start out with lots of extra folders or binders. You will need them to accumulate articles in reading-intensive courses, and you are much more likely to stick with your organizing routine if you have the supplies you need close at hand.
- Create a directory system on your computer to keep track of your course work as well as other documents and data that you might collect throughout the term.
  - » Note that within the file "Versions of Paper," a version numbering system is being applied. You can make up a system that works for you. Some people like to use a version numbering system based on dates. For example, the file might be called "Initial Draft.March.15.06." Every so often, leave a version as it is. That is, copy the file and rename it with the next version number. Use the newest version when you begin to make

more improvements to the paper. This way, if you don't like the direction you took in the version you are working on, or if you corrupt it somehow, you can go back to the prior version and start afresh.

- All work stored on a hard drive needs to be backed up because hard drives can fail. Every week or so, write your most important and active files to a CD. When you do this, use a name that indicates what you have saved and the date you saved it, for example, "Course_Work_Backup/15/03/06." Use a CD marker to write the saved file name on the top of the disc. As you can imagine, after you do this for a while, you end up with a stack of backup discs. Labelling them properly will help you keep them all straight, and help you avoid wasting time later if you need to refer to a particular saved item.

- If you are working on something that is particularly important with an approaching due date, back up more often, such as every hour or so. Some people keep a jump drive plugged in all the time and copy the important work onto it every now and then. If you do this, make sure you revert back to your hard drive when you begin working on the paper again. It can be a real mess if you work from and save onto the jump drive for an hour or so, and then when you pick up the work a few hours later, you open the version that is on your hard drive and work on it for a while. One way to avoid this is to always work from and save onto the hard drive. When you back up onto the jump drive, use "save as" to do so. When the save onto the jump drive is completed, use "save as" immediately thereafter to save onto the hard drive. If you make this a habit, you will avoid the messy mismatch referred to above.

Use an accordion file, also known as an expandable folder, to store notes, papers and articles that you collect. This is useful to keep all your personal folders orderly and will help you find information quickly. It is just as easy to pop a piece of paper into a folder as it is to stuff it into a drawer. The difference with the former is that you can find it again.

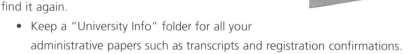

- Keep a "University Info" folder for all your administrative papers such as transcripts and registration confirmations.
- Keep a "University Info—Brochures" folder for the various frosh week information packages, handouts and brochures you will receive.

- Keep a "Personal Info" folder for medical papers and documents such as your tax returns.
- Keep bills and proof of payment in an "Expenses" folder. If you pay your bills on-line, write the payment confirmation number on your bill or print out the on-line confirmation, and staple it to the bill.
- Keep a "House Info" folder for your lease and utility payments in case you need to query something with your landlord.
- Keep receipts handy in a "Purchases" folder in case you need to return an item such as a textbook. A receipt may be necessary to claim on a guarantee if an item breaks.
- Set up additional folders as the need arises, for such things as car expenses or insurance. The idea is to use a folder-based system to keep track of the many bits and pieces of paper that will very likely appear with considerable frequency.

Staying organized is a life skill that reduces stress and frees up more time for enjoyable activities.

NOTES

Academic Skills

• • •

Academic Skills

You might think that after so many years in school prior to university, you have the learning game down pat. But university is different. You are seriously on your own when it comes to your own learning agenda, and there will be much more information coming at you than you are used to. This is not to say it isn't fun. It is! After all, you get to choose what you study, and you have the freedom to learn in your own way and when it suits you. The point is there are a number of things you can do to make yourself more effective, and that's important. We have recorded some of them in this section.

Biggest Challenges
- Going to every class
- Procrastination
- Developing regular study habits
- Keeping motivated, even when the professor is boring or the course content is not interesting
- Asking for help

6. Good Study Habits Don't Come Naturally

The act of studying is a skill, and like all skills it has to be learned. To succeed you have to practice and apply this skill. The fact that you have already been in school and successful for years doesn't necessarily mean that you are good at studying. You may have been getting by on strategies that worked at the high school level that will let you down badly at university where the pace and complexity are a leap above those found at most high schools. This is your opportunity to develop critical thinking skills and improve your communication skills. Reflect on how much you really know about studying. Think about how much of this you have really put into practice, and think about what changes you have to make to truly get you what you want out of your university experience.

6.1   The right study environment

Deciding where you study is more important than you may realize. You need to be able to concentrate and learn course material without anything else competing for your attention. Be honest with yourself about how well you can ignore distractions.

- At the very beginning of term, find a quiet, well-lit place to study where there is nothing to distract you, and where you are unlikely to run into friends. Get into the habit of going there to work all the time.
- If you are easily distracted, try to isolate yourself from possible interruptions, or temptations to take "short breaks" to do something else.
  - » You may think being alone in your room is the answer. However, consider whether your roommate will be around, whether the phone might ring, whether a friend might knock on the door or whether you will be tempted to play "just 20 minutes" of your favourite computer or video game. If so, your room is not the best place to study;
  - » Perhaps the library is the answer. Guess what? Most other students will have had the same thought. Unless you know you can ignore the opportunity to have a quick chat with your friends, you should not go there either unless you are disciplined enough to hide in a secluded corner and resist taking walks to see who's around;
  - » Seek out an empty classroom or go to a different faculty building to find a

secluded spot so you will be less likely to run into your friends. It may even be wise to refrain from publicizing this location;

» It will likely take you less time to complete your studying or other work in a quiet environment than it will in more disruptive surroundings.

- Decide if you study better in complete silence or prefer some soft music or other background sound. Test it out. Use headphones on a low volume so as not to bother others around you.

You may prefer to study with background noise. Remember that you will have to write exams in silence so you may wish to practice working in silence as exam time approaches.

Erin, University of Toronto, Arts '04

Some students believe they study better in the company of others.

- If you live in residence or a busy house and cannot ignore tempting distractions, make sure you find a better study location, such as the library or a lounge.
- If you feel that you absorb more by bouncing ideas off a study buddy, ensure you pick someone who has the same level of commitment so you are not faced with any temptation to slack off.
- If you decide to work with a study buddy, put some formality into the arrangement so it doesn't dissolve into a recurrent social event. For example, agree to study something specific for two hours and then get together to discuss what you studied. Then repeat the process.

6.2   When should you study?

Determine the time of day when you are most receptive to learning.

- Are you a "morning person" or a "night owl"? When are you most alert and energetic? Choose that time to do the tasks that take the most thought and creativity. Few people truly do better doing university-level work late at night.
- Leave the more routine tasks for your less productive time.
- Don't sit down to study until you have eaten a nutritious meal, whether it be breakfast, lunch or dinner. Have some healthy snacks on hand if you plan to work for more than a few hours. Refer to Chapter 13.3.
- Cramming late at night on a caffeine high is not a productive way to function, especially if you do this the night before a test or exam. It will result in a poor night's sleep, leaving you less able to cope with any unforeseen

challenges the next day. This is bad news if a wacky question shows up on the test or exam!

Despite the best intentions, an all-nighter is inevitable at least once during the year. Just don't make it a habit.

Zoe, Queen's University, ArtSci '08

6.3   Know your learning style

Everyone learns in a way that is unique. Almost always, people use a combination of learning approaches. Think about how you learn best, and adopt strategies to reinforce your primary learning strength.

- Auditory learners learn best by hearing information. They prefer to discuss their ideas with friends and work in study groups, or record lectures to listen to after class and repeat what they are trying to learn...also known as "talking to yourself."
- Visual / Nonverbal learners absorb information by seeing it in a picture or design. They learn best with the use of diagrams, charts, concept maps and by highlighting text.
- Visual / Verbal learners learn best from information presented in writing and benefit from the use of the blackboard and PowerPoint presentations. Using flash cards may be helpful to trigger memory. They can "see" the material as it was laid out on the page.
- Kinesthetic learners often like to move their bodies as they absorb information, for example, jiggling their knee, tapping their foot or wiggling in their chair. They like to "learn by doing" by using a hands-on approach, and will learn easily from hands-on experiments. Pacing around the room or playing with a stress ball helps them to concentrate.

Exploit your strongest learning style, but also practice other strategies to develop your learning capabilities, and to support and enhance your understanding of the material. Virtually all of us learn best by using more than one approach in combination.

- Know yourself and don't be swayed by what your peers need to do, or say they need to do, to succeed.
  - » Just because your friend can absorb the material in a chapter after reading it once does not mean you will be able to;
  - » Peers sometimes understate what they are doing to avoid looking too

serious or boring! If you model your behaviour on what your colleagues "say" they are doing, you could be studying much less than they are and you could well be studying far too little.

Professors are often asked, "What should I do to do well in your course?" There is both a short answer and a long answer to this question. The short answer is that there are three things you need to do: 1) keep up, 2) keep up, and 3) keep up. You get the idea! The long answer is pretty similar to the short answer, and is grounded in two principles.

The first principle is that most of us learn better when we invoke several learning techniques. That is "read it, hear it, reflect upon it, and do it" works better than any one or two approaches by themselves.

The second principle is that keeping up is essential. Most of us do not truly "learn" when we are scrambling to catch up or to get something done within a time frame that is far too short for the work at hand. Most of us do not truly "learn" if we are overridden by anxiety from any source, but even more so if the source of our anxiety is the fact that we have neglected some course work and are now behind.

So the long answer is: use multiple learning techniques, and keep up!

6.4   Procrastination

> **I can** resist anything but temptation.
> Oscar Wilde

It is easy to ignore your studies in favour of distracting activities such as playing video games, watching TV, organizing your room or hanging out with friends. Often these represent an avoidance technique, rather than a sincere desire to engage in these activities.

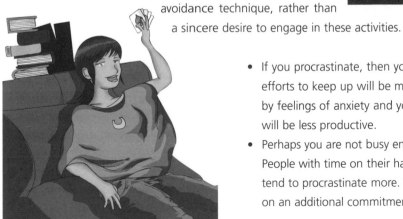

- If you procrastinate, then your efforts to keep up will be marred by feelings of anxiety and you will be less productive.
- Perhaps you are not busy enough. People with time on their hands tend to procrastinate more. Take on an additional commitment,

such as volunteering for an hour or two, and keep busy. It may be easier for you to get everything done when you know time is limited. You will probably feel better too!

- Understand that procrastination is a kind of mental inertia—a mind at rest tends to stay at rest; a force must be applied to change from a state of rest to a state of action. This is where you come in. You apply "the force"!

- Start a task by breaking it down into manageable pieces and complete the first step. Once you get going it is much easier to stay motivated and complete your work. You will be surprised by what you can accomplish and how good you feel.

- After studying, reward yourself with enjoyable activities.

6.5   Stay organized

Use your *University Matters Student Planner* to manage your time and stay ahead of deadlines. Refer to Chapter 5.

Your university professors will not be coordinating the due dates of assignments with each other, so you must be prepared for an influx of work from different courses that must be submitted during the same week, or even on the same day. Some professors will move due dates when advised of multiple demands, but most will not. This is not inflexibility or insensitivity on the part of the professor. It is a reflection of the reality that an alternate date will probably cause the same problems, but for a different sub-set of students.

- Don't lose marks by handing work in late due to poor planning. Your marks, after all, should reflect your learning.

Resist the urge to defer studying, writing papers or reviewing for exams until a few days before they are due.

- You may be faced with a family emergency or come down with a cold, the flu or some other illness just as you come up against an important deadline.

- Although you may qualify for a doctor's note that will allow you to submit work or write a test at a later date, it is never fun to have to do this. It is better to be prepared and avoid this situation unless you absolutely have no choice.

Save your work frequently on your computer as you go, especially when completing important assignments. Refer to Chapter 5.4.

> **Make** saving your work a habit, or better yet, set your computer to prompt you to auto-save very frequently.

- Most professors will be unsympathetic to claims that you have lost your work, couldn't print your work, or couldn't recover saved data when you brought your work in for printing, etc. The problem is that professors cannot distinguish between legitimate bad luck and bad planning, so there is little choice but to treat them all as the latter.

If your field of study requires you to read a large number of articles, summarize them as you go along.

- Record in a Word document on your computer the proper citation for each article. Use the citation format your professor requires. Refer to Chapter 2.9 for some popular styles.
- Underneath the citation, make the notes you need to summarize the article, or to enable you to study and use content from the article in your papers. Typically you can cut and paste material from your notes into the main body of your paper. Make sure you cite papers properly to avoid plagiarism.
- Nowadays, many sources that you are likely to cite in a paper will be Web addresses. Determine at the outset of your work your professor's preferred approach to citing material from the Web.
- When you need the list of references for your paper, copy the file of citations and notes into the references section of your paper. Delete all the notes and any citations not used in the paper. What is left is your list of references.
- Keep the file with both the notes and citations recorded on it for future studying or reference when writing other papers.
- Keep and file all the papers you have read. You may need one or more of them at a later date. Keep them with the printed version of the paper you wrote.
- Print and file the printed copy of all electronic materials such as news articles and Web sources as they may change frequently or be taken down from Web sites without notice, and may not be accessible when you need them at a later date.

6.6   Don't get hung up on marks

You might be shocked at the difference between your marks at university and your graduating average from high school. Many students are. Many factors contribute to this phenomenon:

On average, marks tend to be twenty percentage points lower. Yes, that's right! If you were getting 90s in high school, don't be surprised if you get 70s in university.

- The university professor's job is to deliver to students the material set out in the course outline. It is your responsibility to learn it. A high school teacher, on the other hand, generally shares somewhat more responsibility with you to make sure the material is "learned";
- Some universities enforce a bell curve, or at least specify a typical distribution and require professors to explain deviations from the specified distribution to avoid having too many As. This has the effect of pushing most of the class down into the B+ and below range. Some schools seek to limit the number in the B+ and above range, which has the effect of pushing a large chunk of the class into the B and B- ranges or below[36]. It is easy to predict the effect this has on class averages, and averages of individual students;
- Higher academic standards exist at university;
- Class average marks are often mentioned, but sometimes are not particularly meaningful. The case can arise where a few students do extremely well while most do poorly. The few excellent marks pull the average up and make it unrepresentative of how most students performed;
- Some believe there is grade inflation in the high school environment. High schools are under pressure to increase the acceptance rate of their students into universities; higher marks result in higher acceptance rates.

High school students are motivated to pick reputed "bird courses," or to select a course section with teachers who are reputed to give higher grades.
Ottawa Citizen, May 3, 2005, Mark 'Inflation' Skews G12 Results

Use your mark as an indicator of how well you understood and met the professor's expectations. Some professors may only give an A to the top two or three students.

---

36   Although the correspondence of numerical grades to letter grades varies somewhat by university, a typical B- range is 70-72, and a typical B range is 73-76. c.f. Carleton University Undergraduate Calendar, 2004-05, Section 2.3, downloaded from http://www.carleton.ca/cuuc/regulations/acadregs2.html#23, April 16, 2005.

I, and so many others that I knew, were surprised to find that U of T was not handing out A grades like our high schools had been doing. In high school, getting an A, being a top student, seemed to have been as easy as breathing…a matter of minimal effort. I think many, many people find it very depressing when they can no longer meet the same standard so easily attainable before.

For all of its enlightenment, for all of its sense of community, a university still suffers under a bureaucracy, and is still weighed down by many biases. A lot of very intelligent people do not excel in the university structure, and are made to feel as though they are not as good as those who do. I found this to be the hardest thing to accept.

Katrina, University of Toronto, Art History '04

If you are unsure of how to interpret your mark, ask for input from your professor.

- Typically marks improve as you advance through your program.
- Assess your performance with the following in mind:
  - » How much effort did I put in?
  - » How tough were the questions?
  - » Have I learned more than my marks reflect?
- In theory, your mark should reflect the degree to which you have mastered the material presented in the course. Tests and exams are meant to test your level of mastery. Remember this when you review your marks. Can you really expect to get 90 percent if you have only thoroughly studied 65 percent of the material?

Twenty-seven percent of first-year students report a grade point average of C+ or lower, compared with 14 percent of students in fourth year.[37]

- Remember that a university education tells future employers that you have the discipline to learn, meet deadlines, and work with others. Your degree in hand, a track record of volunteer and extracurricular activities, together with a positive attitude, are more important than each individual mark.
- Think positively and take steps to improve any unsatisfactory marks if you have underperformed.
- Do not interpret marks as a measure of your self-worth.
- It is difficult to gauge the relationship between marks and effort. Be careful about mapping out a study plan that targets a middle-of-the-road mark. Some students find that if they work very hard they can get an A, but if they

---

37 Survey of Undergraduate University Students: University of Winnipeg, 2002, downloaded from http://www.uwinnipeg.ca/index/cms-filesystem-action?file=pdfs/future/cusc.pdf on April 6, 2005.

back off on the effort a little bit, the slippage can be dramatic, sometimes to a C or worse.

6.7   Reading week

Before you get too excited about the prospect of an entire week without classes, let us point out that you only get a reading week in the second term. In today's world, where there are so many half-courses, it is difficult to understand why there is a reading week in  one term and not the other. In the days when most courses were full-year courses, reading week was a time to regroup after about nineteen weeks of classes, and to put in some intensive work on papers due at the end of the course.

This period of time allows you to re-energize and to review your work for mid-term exams and tests, to complete papers, and to catch up.

- A break from schoolwork is nice, but be honest with yourself. How much time do you really need for rest and fun?
- Be careful about establishing your own approach to reading week based on the messages others are sending out.
  » Some who say they are blowing off academic work for the entire week actually aren't. If you waste all of reading week, you may be doing a lot less work than these people, and a lot less than you actually need to do;
  » Some have worked hard to get ahead of schedule before reading week and can afford to take a more relaxed approach. Are you in the same boat?
  » Some have lower performance standards than you do, and don't mind gaining relaxation time at the expense of marks. Is this your attitude as well?
  » Make a choice that is right for you given your workload and aspirations. If doing a reasonable amount of work during reading week is socially awkward for you, remember that no one but you needs to know.
- Keeping on top of your academic work now will enable you to keep everything balanced later.

- If you follow the week-to-week study protocol as suggested in Chapter 7, you should be able to relax, re-energize, and only do a bit of work. Use the Study Protocol Worksheet in your *University Matters Student Planner* or download a copy from www.universitymatters.ca.
- If mid-term exams are scheduled for the week after reading week, you really should devote a good chunk of your time to studying. Schedule your time well during reading week and you will still have time to relax.
- If you have fallen behind, put your nose to the grindstone, avoid distractions and position yourself to start the last six weeks of the academic year in good shape. Putting in a tough week of work to convert these weeks from misery to enjoyment is a good trade-off. Go for it!

Remember there will be lots of opportunities for fun after your exams, but you only have one shot to meet your academic priorities in the few remaining weeks between reading week and the end of term.

- As many students do, you might want to use reading week to return home to look for a job for the summer.
  - » Make sure your resume is current and reflects any new skills you have developed at university. Refer to the Resume Builder Worksheet in your *University Matters Student Planner* or download a copy from www.universitymatters.ca
  - » Your university will have a Career Centre that focuses on employment opportunities for graduating students. It may have some summer jobs posted, and will certainly have resources to help you improve the key messages in your resume. Your resume is important because it distinguishes you from the many other students seeking a summer job;
  - » Check out your university's career planning centre Web site for additional resources. York University has an award-winning site offering tips on resume writing and interviewing skills. Visit it at www.yorku.ca/careers/cyberguide
- If you have kept up with your work and have the financial resources, plan ski holidays or vacations to the sunny south to rest and recharge your batteries. Before you book:
  - » Think Last Minute Club. Do not book a vacation until at least three weeks beforehand to ensure you are on top of your academic work. Check the following sites for cheap flights:
    www.travelocity.ca
    www.expedia.ca

» Ensure you have written all the dates for tests, submissions and other course requirements in your *University Matters Student Planner* and that you have blocked out the time required to meet those commitments. Then you know you can complete all of your academic work.

7. A Week-to-Week Study Protocol

7.1 Establish a routine

Think of each day as a "workday." Most courses are structured with the expectation you will spend at least two hours doing course-related work for each hour of class time. Add to that papers and projects and you will appreciate the need to keep up with your work. Use the Study Protocol Worksheet in your *University Matters Student Planner* or download a copy from www.universitymatters.ca.

On average, students report spending 16 hours a week in classes and labs, and 17 hours a week on academic work outside class and labs. These same students report an average mark between a B and a B+. A typical student reports completing 11 papers or reports in the school year.[38]

- You can see from the data referred to in the box above that you can easily exceed the average student's effort and, if it is important to you, gain competitive advantage by allocating the expected two hours of study time for each hour of class time.
- Get into the routine of getting up and going to bed at the same time each day.
  - » Check your *University Matters Student Planner* for your day's commitments;
  - » Be disciplined about using non-class time to meet your academic commitments with planned breaks to socialize with friends.
- Get going right away! If you start reading early in the term and keep ahead, you will quickly shift into a comfortable routine without anxiety.
- Get started on large assignments. There are two approaches to doing this.
  - » Some people prefer to take the bull by the horns and jump right into the most challenging piece of work they have. If that's you, then great!

---

38 Survey of Undergraduate University Students: University of Winnipeg, 2002, downloaded from http://www.uwinnipeg.ca/index/cms-filesystem-action?file=pdfs/future/cusc.pdf on April 6, 2005.

» Others find this daunting; they procrastinate and end up doing nothing until they are almost out of time! If that's you, start with a few of the short, easy tasks. You will feel a sense of accomplishment completing them. Then tackle some of the larger tasks. If they seem overwhelming, break them down further into smaller more manageable pieces.

- Take short refresher breaks. A brisk ten-minute walk will do wonders to refresh your mind.
- If you are studying late at night and are having difficulty absorbing the material, go to bed. Set your alarm and get up after you have had a healthy amount of sleep. A good night's sleep will refresh your brain and you will be able to focus much better in the morning. Refer to Chapter 13.1.

7.2   Before class

Refer to your course outline frequently, not just on the first day of class when it is handed out. Looking at what you have done in the preceding weeks serves as a refresher of what course material has been covered, and also helps put the upcoming material in context. The course outline also spells out what you have to read and do through to the end of the course.

- Read the relevant chapters before class.
- Develop a reading strategy to focus first on what is most relevant or most important.
- If time permits the luxury of additional reading, by all means, read more.
- One obvious, but rarely verbalized point: it is very difficult to speed up reading; so if you fall behind there is no sense in which you can "sprint" to catch up. Each hour of reading lost early on truly translates into an hour of reading later in the term, possibly when you can least afford it.
- Most people find it helpful to use a highlighter for key words or phrases.

Completing the assigned readings is the task students neglect most often. But keeping current is so important because it alleviates the overwhelming stress that can hit as assignments flow in and you realize you have fallen significantly behind.

- Make a note of things that are not clear to you from the readings. This puts you in a better position to use lecture time to ask questions about what you don't understand. It also helps avoid the problem of assuming that an unclear comment in class "will be explained in the text," when in fact it might not be.
- Some professors expect students to have read and absorbed the relevant chapters before class and will teach around the subject matter in class accordingly. It is always nice if the professor tells you of this requirement, but not all do, and you can get caught out if you haven't done the reading. In some cases, this can make the lecture unintelligible, which presents problems:
  - » First, it will be abundantly clear to you that you have just fallen behind. You have to catch up on the reading *and* the lecture that you have just "missed."
  - » Second, and more immediate, the lecture will be a painful and discouraging experience;
  - » Third, if called upon in class, your shortcomings will be obvious, possibly embarrassing you, and could cost you class participation marks.
- Some professors post lecture notes on their course Web sites. Print them off before class, skim through them and bring them to class. You will be able to listen better and make supplementary notes to enhance your understanding.
- Skim your notes from the previous class to ensure you remember where the professor left off when the lecture ended. Some professors remind students about where they left off as a way of linking the classes together, but some don't. It can be very confusing if the professor launches into new material and you are unable to put it into context.

7.3   The obvious? Go to class!

In the high school environment, going to class is pretty firmly entrenched in the culture, and absenteeism is monitored and quickly addressed.

Eighty-two percent of university students say they skip class once a week or more.[39]

---

39   c. f. Who pursues postsecondary education, who leaves and why: Results from the Youth in Transition Survey. Statistics Canada, Catalogue no. 81-595-MIE – No. 026.

- At university, with larger classes, first-year university students are completely anonymous and there are no visible penalties arising from missing classes.
- You may be surprised at how difficult it is to get motivated to go to class, especially the larger classes, and how easy it is to convince yourself that you are not "missing that much" and can easily "catch up." But the opposite is often true. Missing classes sets you up for achieving poorer grades.
- Although students do skip classes, not doing so is the most prominent piece of advice experienced students give to First Years.

An informal survey was conducted in a class of 49 students. They were asked to write down three pieces of advice for new students. The top piece of advice from 55 percent of the students was "always go to class."

- Once you have skipped a class or two, you may feel that:
  » You have fallen behind so you are doomed;
  » You have not "missed that much" and can make it up.
- In reality, neither conclusion is absolutely correct. If you have missed a couple of classes, you aren't doomed—but you aren't exactly in great shape. Your only alternative is to put your head down and work hard until you feel you are on top of your work. It often takes more time to catch up than if you'd gone to the class in the first place.

Attend all lectures and participate in class, because lots of professors give you participation marks when you attend class. Those marks, which are referred to as "easy," are some of the marks that are really important to get. They can be the difference between a pass and a fail, or 78 percent and 82 percent. Don't ever skip classes!

Tomo, University of Guelph, Business Administration '07

- Professors tend to notice who attends class and who doesn't. It is possible that a professor will be inclined to go out of his way to help students who appear to be trying hard, but not others. Most professors will not be favourably impressed if you have not attended class regularly, and then attempt to use office hours or a flood of e-mail inquiries at the end of term as a substitute.

I was surprised to find that a lot of things I had always thought myself to be passionate about did not actually translate into things I wanted to study. For that reason, I found a lot of introductory courses boring and difficult to attend. My biggest failure in university was that I did not put the effort into classes I found boring and often stopped attending lectures, or handing in smaller assignments, and did very poorly in those instances as a result. It wasn't until I gained a sense of what I really wanted to do, or at least took it upon myself to drop a class when it was hopelessly uninteresting, that I put a halt to terrible results.

Katrina, University of Toronto, Art History '04

- Listen well and take concise notes in class.
- Although the same material may be in the text, attending class will reinforce the content in your memory, and the professor's comments should serve to enhance the relevancy and your learning experience.
- Listen for such professorial comments as "This is key" and "This is an important concept…" and asterisk those in your notes.

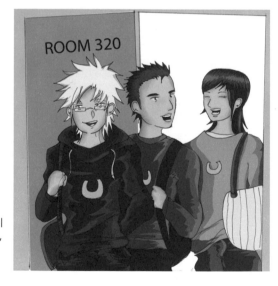

- If you prefer, and the professor is agreeable, use a recording device. This is useful for clarifying specific points later, but will take longer to completely review as compared to studying your notes.
- Ask questions in class.
  - » You can be sure that a number of other students in the class have the same question on their minds. Questions are just as important as answers to both the students and the professor. They are a way to enable the

professor to identify the concepts you don't understand and lead to additional explanation for everyone in the class;

» If you don't understand some of the material, go down to the front of the room right after the class and tell the professor you have some questions. He or she may be able to make a couple of quick comments that completely clear things up for you, or be able to direct you to some material, or other solution, that will help you. That is why the professor is there;

» Smaller classes may have a participation mark component. Students who show up and ask good questions get remembered and usually ace this.

• Professors want you to devote your time to the course material that is difficult and/or important, and to master this material. It is not unusual for professors to target this material for examination. If you go to class and listen well, you may be able to deduce some of what will be on the next test or exam.

• If you have to miss a class due to illness, get a copy of the notes from two classmates as soon as possible, and review the missed work. Refer to Chapter 4.4. See the professor or teaching assistant for an explanation of any part of the material you don't understand. The professor will be responsive if he or she sees you are on top of your work. If you delay trying to catch up until right before an exam, you may not get as helpful a response.

7.4 After class

Soon after class, preferably within a couple of hours, go to a quiet place and review the notes you took in class. Annotate them where they are unclear or too sketchy.

• You probably use your own personal version of note-taking shorthand. If you are like most of us, it probably isn't perfect, so there may be entries in your notes that won't make a lot of sense to you ten weeks later when you are studying for the final.

• If you look at your notes right after class you will probably be able to recall the point you were trying to capture and can make a clarifying comment right then and there.

---

40   c. f. Who pursues postsecondary education, who leaves and why: Results from the Youth in Transition Survey. Statistics Canada, Catalogue no. 81-595-MIE – No. 026.

- For important and more complex points, make a note of the page in the text where further detail is provided. Sometimes the professor will even state the page reference in class. This will help when you are reviewing for tests and exams. It also underscores the benefit of having the correct edition of the text.
- This is a good time to make summary notes from your text that will be useful to you when you are studying for tests or the final exam. Develop study notes and jot down the pertinent facts in each chapter using abbreviations rather than full sentences. Reread these notes in three days to see if you have recorded enough detail. This way you will become efficient at summarizing written material you have read.
- Some people use different coloured highlighters to make a visual map of the material the course is covering. The colour coding you do now will help you to see how things fit together when you study for tests or the final exam later on in the term. For example, use one colour for definitions and another for key concepts.
- Make sure you understand what has been covered in class. If you don't:
  » Reread your notes from class. Sometimes a quick reread will show you that you really do understand, or it may be that the solution to your problem is in the notes and you lost track of it in the heat of the moment of taking notes;
  » Reread the assigned chapters. The part of the book that addresses the topic you are having trouble with may make a lot more sense to you after hearing the lecture;
  » Talk with classmates. It is amazing how often an alternate way of expressing a point can make it clear to you;
  » If you are still not clear on something, deal with it right away by going to see your teaching assistant or professor as soon as possible. They often have very effective ways of explaining a point that they didn't use in class because they don't work well in a large group setting, but can be used in a one-on-one setting.

Most importantly, don't accumulate concepts you don't understand. In many courses, later material depends on concepts laid down at the start of the course. If you have a good grasp of them, your developing knowledge will be based on a firm foundation. If you don't, the foundation will be shaky. Invest time early on to make the foundation strong.

- Review assignments as soon as they are given out rather than filing them away until a week before the due date. This way your mind can start pondering the task at hand and you can jot down ideas as they come to you.
  - » Enter the due date in your *University Matters Student Planner*;
  - » Estimate how long the assignment will take by breaking it into smaller pieces and blocking out the required time in your *University Matters Student Planner,* working backwards from the due date. Refer to Chapter 5;

Your professors will likely expect you to present arguments and new ideas in your reports, papers and essays, not just a restatement of already-known facts. Allow your brain "thinking time" to reflect on issues and alternate approaches. Your brain works best when it can "sleep" on a problem for several nights.

  - » Use the time when you are walking to and fro, or riding the bus, to ponder issues and ideas related to papers or projects ahead of you;
  - » When you get assignments back, ensure you understand where you went wrong. Review of assignments is crucial for exam studying and it is much easier to correct errors while the topic is fresh in your mind.
- Do the practice problems at the end of each chapter. Practice does make perfect, or at least closer to it than no practice at all.
- File any loose papers in the appropriate course folders or binders.

7.5 Teaching assistants (TAs) and tutorial sessions

You should attend as many of the tutorial sessions as you can, even if you feel comfortable with the course content.
- Practicing extra questions will reinforce the material.
- Listening to questions from other students will help you assess your depth of understanding.
- TAs can help you manage your time by focusing your studying on the important issues. They can help you identify what the professor is looking for in certain assignments. They are a valuable resource, so use them.
- Some TAs will even proofread your paper and provide additional guidance if you have it ready soon enough in advance of the due date.

- Some professors provide marks for attending tutorials. These are easy marks and also are there to tell you that the professor believes that attending the tutorials and participating are important to your success.

When you have an essay due, make sure you get it done ahead of time, so if you need to, you can go and see your TA for guidance. The TA can help you focus your paper, which will definitely mean improved marks, and less stress because it also means you can't procrastinate as much. If you want the TA to look over your whole essay, it takes about a week, so you need to get it done even earlier. Also, if your campus has a writing centre service, then you need to make an appointment in advance and have the essay done for the staff there to look it over. However, if you just want to meet with your TA and discuss your ideas, or an outline, then you can do that usually up to a couple of days before the essay is due. I've found that it's usually really hard to get an essay done more than a week before the due date, but as I improve my time management skills I suppose it could be possible!

Zoe, Queen's University, ArtSci '08

8. Doing the Work

In this chapter we discuss papers, projects, presentations and exams. These are your academic deliverables. They are the tools professors use to help you to learn, and to assess to what extent you have mastered the required material. Read, think, question and critique: these are your tools. Take presentations, for example. There is nothing quite like the prospect of having to stand up in front of your friends and colleagues to motivate you to do good research, and to put together a good presentation. These deliverables are also opportunities for you to delve into subjects that, hopefully, you want to find out more about. They are opportunities to hone skills that will be very important to you for the rest of your life. Use these opportunities to good advantage.

Sometimes professors provide a lot of direction concerning topics. They may confine the topic to a narrow area because they want you to study and learn about something specific that is important to their course. These are the easy cases. Just follow the instructions, work hard, and you will get a decent paper completed. The more difficult situations are those where the topic requirements are open-ended. This means you have to choose a topic. The sooner you do this the better.

8.1   Choosing a topic

Determine your topic, at first in general terms. You will naturally fine-tune it as you learn more about the topic. But how do you go about choosing?

Relevance:
- The overriding criterion is that the topic must be a good fit with the professor's stated requirement. Resist the temptation to adopt a topic that is only tangentially related to the requirement because you have a lot of material on it.
  - » Wrong: "I know a lot about topic X so I will contort this topic to fit into the professor's requirements." By the way, even marginally experienced course instructors will see this one from a mile off and judge you accordingly;
  - » Right: "I really understand what the professor requires, and topics A, B and C seem to fit."

Interest:
- It is important to find a topic that interests you. It is much more difficult to apply yourself if you aren't interested in a topic, which can lead to procrastination.
  - » However, there will be occasions when you get an assignment that simply doesn't fit with your interests. This is the time when you just have to knuckle down and get it done.

Scope:
- The most frequent mistake is to specify a topic in such a way that the scope is much too broad. This leads to an impossible research task, and difficulties

getting the paper to fit within the professor's required page or word limit.

» While many students fear long papers, they are actually much easier to write than short papers. This is because it is much easier to ramble on indefinitely, paying no heed to a page or word restriction, and much more difficult to pare a fifteen-page paper down to a ten-page one.

In one course, we used to ask students to do a 15-minute presentation, but we found that most of the presentations ran long and students were complaining about how difficult it was to condense their message to fit the allocated time. When we expanded the limit to 20 minutes the next year, every single group expressed concern about whether they could fill the available time. They need not have worried. On presentation day, every single presentation ran long. This is because it is much easier to ramble than to be concise.

Preliminary research:

• Do a quick check to find out whether or not there is much material on your selected topic in the library or on the Internet.

We once asked students to do a project that involved selecting a country and writing a paper on how its central bank functioned. One student selected a country that interested him and began his work. It wasn't until later that he discovered the central bank's Web site, the prime source of information for the project, was published only in the domestic language of the country. Guess what? It wasn't English! A quick check of logical sources early on would have saved this student a lot of problems.

Sound it out:

• Discuss ideas around your general topic with anyone who will listen. You should be looking for the answers to two questions:
  » Do people seem interested?
  » Do people think there is good information available to you?
• Use your fellow students, friends and family to practice discussing your ideas at various levels.
  » Verbalizing your thoughts will help clarify them for yourself;
  » They may have useful insights. Write them down as they arise.

Search engines:

• Now it is time to hit the electronic search engines. In today's world, there are many powerful research tools available.

» Web-based search engines, such as Google, can be very useful. You will soon see that volumes have been written on an amazing number of topics. This material can be invaluable for guiding your own thinking on your topic. Reading what other people have written on a topic can sometimes lead to new insights for you;

» Periodicals search engines are provided by the library. These search engines are particularly fast and effective and enable you to find articles in academic journals and other periodicals. There are different search engines for different disciplines. If you are in doubt about which one to use, your professor or teaching assistant can usually advise you, as well as the staff at the library. In some cases, these search engines lead to an entire article in electronic form, which can then be saved in your inventory for later reading as part of your intensive research, and as a source for quotes, and so on, as you write your paper;

» Library catalogue search engines are also very effective in that they can lead you to the books and other resources that are relevant to your topic. The books in the library stacks tend to be organized by topic. Once you identify a book you like, go to its location in the stacks and see if there are any other books located in that general area that seem appropriate, but did not show up in your electronic search.

• The key is to get through this stage quickly, as your results will shape your topic going forward.

» Remember that your goal here is not to generate a list of publications that you can use to pad the references section of your paper. Your goal is to find useful and interesting material to read that will help you construct your paper;

» Your professor wants you to find and read good source material so that you will learn about your topic, and be able to write a good paper.

- Be wary of the accuracy of information you find on the net, especially content from little-known sites. Use credible sources, not "Dave's home page."

Fine-tune your topic:
- Use your preliminary reading to fine-tune your topic. As you read, make notes, collect and save graphs, tables of data, pictures and maps, as appropriate. Use jot notes to avoid plagiarism. Save the jot notes and use them later to develop written material in your own voice. Refer to Chapter 6.5 for details of how to summarize articles.
- Do additional reading to test out your fine-tuned topic.
- You can now be more targeted in your literature searches, which is another way of saying you will spend less time reading things that don't contribute to your paper.
- Use the bibliographies from papers already in your inventory to lead you to additional interesting or relevant papers. This helps you to read and research in a targeted way, which can be a real time saver.

8.2 Writing papers

There are many different kinds of courses at university that will require you to write a paper, and there are many different kinds of papers. For instance:
- **Expository:** the requirement is to find out what you can on a topic and record what you have learned;
- **Analytical:** the requirement is to analyze a specific situation and provide a recommended course of action;
- **Creative:** the requirement may be to propose approaches out of the ordinary;
- **Propositional:** you are arguing for or against a stance that you or someone else has taken.

The key is to obtain a clear understanding of the task from your professor.
- Most of the time the professor will spell out the nature of the task in some detail. Pay very close attention when this occurs. This is another very important reason for going to class!
- Make detailed notes of what the professor says. Later, when you are working on the paper, you might find yourself questioning some nuance of the task that may have been answered when the professor addressed the matter in class.

- If you don't think you have a clear understanding, ask your classmates, talk to the professor, or sit down with the TA for clarification. TAs can be excellent resources in this regard, as they have usually taken the same course, sometimes even from the same professor, and have first-hand experience of what it is like to deal with the specific requirement you are facing.

Writing a paper involves a few important steps. Each done well will make the process less time-consuming, and far less painful than otherwise. The outcome will probably be better too! It can be effective to think of writing a paper in terms of bringing the reader along with you on a journey.

- Hopefully you have followed a methodical process to make sure you have a good topic. So now you are ready to get to work. Remember to select an appropriate referencing style as detailed in Chapter 2.8.

Determine what you are going to say in your paper.

- Figure out your "angle" much like a newspaper reporter would.
- Ask yourself, "What is the hook in this that will grab my audience?" Part of the answer lies in the information around the topic itself, but part also lies in how you spin things. Use what seemed to resonate when you spoke to people about your topic.
- What questions do you have about the topic? What questions do you think others might have? Centre on, at most, a few key points or arguments.

Prepare an outline or flow chart using information from what you have read, and what you have concluded from what you have read. Highlight the key messages.

- A flow chart is useful for mapping out your thoughts. Most papers build up from a foundation of basic information and lead to a set of final statements, perhaps even just one main statement. A flow chart records in graphic form how this occurs. It maps out what you need to say, in what order, and the dependencies. That is, if one argument depends on a subsidiary argument or fact, then the subsidiary argument or fact would appear first in the flow chart. Follow the flow chart in the development of your outline and then write the paper from the outline.

Write your paper, using the following guidelines:

- **Introduction:** Set the stage. The reader needs to know what you will be talking about. Make sure you know your audience and what the reader is expecting. Don't be surprised if the paper you eventually write has strayed from your initial introduction. This is quite normal. It is often the case that the initial introduction is useful for getting things going, but as you learn more, the direction of the paper may change. Revisit and, if necessary, rewrite the introduction after you have completed the body of the paper to make sure it is still "in sync" with the paper you have written;

- **Background:** Here is where you can record what you have learned so far about this topic through the readings you have done;

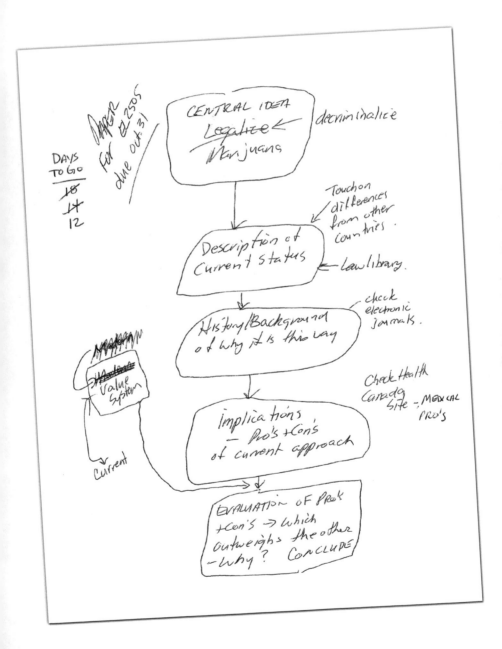

- **Synthesis:** In this part, use what you have already set out in the paper to support the statement(s) you want to make. This can involve using the material in the background as evidence or grounding for your arguments and analysis;
- **Findings:** Now, summarize the statement(s) you want to make;
- **Knit it together:** Complete the first draft of your paper, and begin refining the paper;
- **Feedback:** If time permits, arrange a meeting with your TA for some initial feedback on what you have done;
- **Editing:** Arrange with a friend to edit each other's papers.

Remember to save your work frequently, pretty much every time you pause for thought.

It is much easier to edit an existing paper into a great paper than it is to write a great paper starting from a blank sheet of paper. So get something, dare we say "anything," down on paper because you can't edit what you haven't written!

The occasions when a bibliography or list of references is not required will be rare indeed, possibly non-existent. Develop your bibliography as you go; this means type out the actual citation in proper format when you first go to the source if there is a reasonable likelihood you will refer to that source in your paper. Refer to Chapter 6.5.

- It is much more rewarding to patch in a completed list of references that you created as you worked than it is to construct one from scratch in the late stages of completing a paper. It is easy to delete unwanted references at the last moment, and outright painful to create the list at the last moment when you know your time would be better spent editing your paper, or sleeping if you have just pulled an all-nighter to get it done!

Two aspects of paper writing guaranteed to either drive you crazy or bore you to tears:
- Having to return to the library to retrieve sources for which you forgot to get the correct citation;
- Typing a long list of citations when your paper is completed.

8.3   Projects

Sometimes the requirements for projects are less restrictive than those for papers. If this is the case, then a project is your chance to have fun. If you can, choose a topic you really want to learn about and go after it.

- As with papers, make sure you understand what your professor is looking for.
- Follow the comments pertaining to topic selection in Chapter 8.1.
- The sequencing of your project's development is similar to the approach for doing papers. Follow the steps as detailed in Chapter 8.2.

8.4   Presentations

PRESENTATION

As you learn, you are expected to gain knowledge of various subject areas, as well as develop various skills and competencies. Presentations in front of your peers involve both. Your future employer may not care about particular topics you have researched and presented, but he or she will care that you know how to do thorough research and that you can present effectively.

Presentation of work to others brings up the sometimes-terrifying topic of speaking in public. There are two main themes in this regard:

- The first has to do with overcoming the natural nervousness that comes with public speaking;
- The second has to do with presentation technique, or in other words, how to present effectively.

On the matter of nervousness:

- Most of us grossly overestimate the extent to which the audience is actually paying attention.
  - » We feel as if they are riveted to us, hanging on our every word, and able to detect even the slightest miscue. All of this leads to nervousness completely out of proportion to the nature of the event. Realize one very important thing: they aren't. Few of us are so captivating. It is more or less just you and

a fraction of the crowd at any one point in time. Moreover, it is not even the same fraction of the crowd as you progress through your presentation.

- Breathe.
  - » This has an amazing effect on your ability to function in front of a crowd. Speaking requires at least some air; so does your body. Feed it some air;
  - » Practice deep breathing by placing your hand on your abdomen and feeling it rise and fall.
- Keep organized. Use cue cards.
  - » The fear of losing your train of thought, or losing your place in a talk can be overwhelming;
  - » If you do lose your place, go back to a point in the talk where you knew where you were. This will undoubtedly lead to repetition of some portion of your presentation. Some of the crowd won't notice and the rest will conclude you are repeating yourself for emphasis. So backtrack and carry on as if nothing happened.
- Practice.
  - » Find an empty room with the required presentation equipment, such as a data projector or overhead projector, and say your entire presentation out loud. If you can get a couple of friends to listen and offer advice, so much the better. If you can't, do it by yourself;
  - » Thinking your presentation through in your head is no substitute for this. For one thing, it doesn't require you to practice your breathing in the same way that delivery out loud does;
  - » If you can, practice in the same room you will use for the actual presentation;
  - » If you can't, then scout out the room before you do your presentation. Go right into the room and stand at the podium, or the location from which you will eventually speak. This gives you an idea of what things will look like to you as you present. It will look strange and unfamiliar at first. Best to deal with this when no one is there, rather than in front of the audience when you have other things on your mind.
- If you do make a significant mistake try not to turn the mistake into a riveting performance.
  - » Most of the time a faux pas is much more interesting than the actual content of the speech;
  - » You can either magnify the miscue or make it quietly go away. It all depends on your reaction;
  - » A matter-of-fact reaction can get you out of a lot of situations. It is the

over-reaction that becomes interesting, and that you want to avoid. Few things are as riveting or as uncomfortable to an audience as the prospect of the speaker becoming completely unhinged. Don't give it to them! It's your choice.

Following the usual polite introduction, the speaker strode to the podium, took a confident moment to survey the audience, and then, somewhat theatrically, whisked a bottle of water from the table at her side up to about chest level with the intention of taking its cap off. What she didn't know was that the organizers had already done this for her, and had cleverly rested the cap on top of the open bottle. Why someone thought this was a good idea we will never know, but they did. Water flew out of the bottle and liberally soaked her blouse. I can think of some natural reactions to this that would be quite riveting for the audience. For example, shouting out a few four-letter words, throwing the bottle at the organizers, and storming off the stage. This very composed person quietly said, "Excuse me, I'll be right back." And she was. After a brief few minutes with some paper towels, she proceeded with her presentation quite successfully.

- If you are afraid of public speaking, you should practice as often as possible in non-threatening environments.
  - » Join Toastmasters if public speaking is an important skill in your area of study. Toastmasters is dedicated to improving communication and leadership skills in a supportive environment:
    - » There is probably a club on campus;
    - » You can join a club off-campus if you prefer a non-student environment;
    - » Check their Web site for the nearest club. www.toastmasters.org
  - » Get involved with student union groups, which present you with the opportunity to speak;
  - » Join a drama club;
  - » If you do not have confidence in your ideas, practice by discussing them with someone;
  - » Finally, practice, practice, practice in front of your mirror.

The following are some tips for an effective presentation:
- Your goal is to achieve credibility with the audience. You are not a "deliverer of information," you are a "credible ally of the audience." You need to

connect with the audience and deliver your message. You must achieve and maintain this status if you want people to listen to you;

- Your presentation begins when your name is called:
  » In other words, don't leave your seat and carry on as if no one was watching as you approach the stage, and then try to assume your "presentation persona" once you get behind the podium. As soon as the audience knows who you are, you are "on stage." Act like it;
- Dress in a way that does not undermine your credibility:
  » Show respect for your audience by dressing in a way that is consistent with your role. If you dress in any other way, you are signaling to the audience that you don't care about your message. They won't either!
- Get yourself organized at the podium and don't look at the audience until you are ready:
  » When you are ready, look up, survey the audience, make eye contact with them, and begin. This is a good start;
  » A common error is to look up, survey the audience, pause, and then look back down

> **A maxim for** presenters: "Tell them what you are going to say, say it, tell them what you said!"

  again to do some more shuffling of your papers. This is a "false start." The result is that you lose the connection with the audience. Also, now the audience can't tell from your actions whether you are going to begin, or whether it is just another false start, so it is hard to "get them back." Once you do, it is called a rough start. But at least now you are underway;
- Don't be afraid to pause. Speaking too quickly and never stopping to breathe shows nervousness. You can also faint from this, which is a bad thing;
- If the presentation is a long one, let the audience know where you are in the schedule. Remind them about what you are doing and where you are going with your presentation;
  » Make a few key points rather than attempting to convey everything you know;
  » Remember, they probably aren't paying 100 percent attention, 100 percent of the time, so they need your help;
- Use overheads to guide the audience through your presentation rather than to disclose content. Exceptions to this rule are:
  » Tables and graphs. It takes quite a long time for the audience to read all the headings or axis definitions, so walk them through the graph or table before getting to the conclusions you want them to draw from the information. In other words, spend a bit of time getting the audience

in a position to work with the tables or graphs, then make your point;

» Cartoons, quotes or phrases can be fun to include in a presentation. Just let them pop up and allow the audience time to read and absorb them;

» Keep the text-load on overheads light:

  » Discuss three points at most per slide;

  » Use short phrases, not full sentences;

  » Resist the urge to use funny noises, beeps and whistles on slide transitions. Once may be acceptable, but only if there is a reason for doing so that is clear from the context;

  » Be careful with excessive artistic expression. Too much colour, action, design and artwork can implicitly suggest to the audience that you are using sizzle to compensate for lack of substance. It can also be distracting and hard to follow.

» Limit the number of overheads to something reasonable. Somewhere between one per minute to one every two minutes;

» The use of a couple of props and tools can make a presentation more interesting, but don't overdo it;

» Work from memory as best you can. Reading from the overheads signals that you don't know your material, which undermines your credibility with the audience. It also signals that there is no value-added to you actually being there, as the audience doesn't need your help to read the overheads. You should use the overheads to keep the audience on track. Your job is to deliver additional material orally that relates to the bullet-points on the overhead;

» Facing your audience maintains your connection with them. Inexplicably, the screens on which overheads are projected seem to have a gravitational pull all of their own. We have observed speakers who do well at the beginning of a presentation, but as it unfolds, spend more and more time looking at the screen until at the end they almost have their backs to the audience. Resist the temptation to go through your entire presentation staring back at the projection screen or electronic board;

» Most audiences will forgive and forget if you use index cards. They don't seem to have the same negative connotation as standing with your back to the audience and reading from the screen. It is better if you don't use

> **Never present** something the audience can't see from their seats. This just tells the audience you don't care enough about the message to deliver it properly. They will quickly conclude they shouldn't either.

them, but it is not terminal to your presentation if you do. Knowing you have the flow of information handy if you panic may boost your confidence:

» If you use cue cards, use a highlighter and capitalize key words or phrases so you can glance down and see the next point easily;

» Number the cards. Ever dropped thirty of them on the floor and tried to resume gracefully?

» Don't overload the cards. Better to have a little thicker pile, than densely covered cards;

» Use cards rather than larger sheets of paper. If you are nervous, the larger sheets tremble to such an extent the audience will pay more attention to this than to your ideas;.

We once assigned a presentation to a class that had been split into six groups. Five groups realized that the goal was to do a corporate boardroom-style presentation. The sixth group addressed the topic by way of a very interesting "skit." They all dressed up in, believe it or not, baby diapers, soothers and blankets. You can imagine the contrast with the other groups, not to mention the embarrassment of all concerned.

• Get a clear idea of the qualitative nature of the presentation. You will want the style of your presentation to measure up against those of the other presenters;

• You are on stage until you have seated yourself again.

8.5   Lab reports

The good news here is that in most courses, and almost all first-year courses, the purpose of the lab will be clearly specified for you. Most often, the professor or TA will direct you to a lab manual or provide a handout before you are scheduled to appear in the lab. Your job is to do what is specified.

• The professor or TA will very likely instruct you on how to prepare a lab report, and tell you what they want it to contain. Pay close attention because a failure to comply will cost you marks.

• It might be tempting to take comfort from the fact that the lab manual or handout is there to guide you, and ignore the lab until you show up to perform the work. Don't! Make sure you have a basic understanding of the theory underlying the lab, and the procedure you are to follow. Think through what is supposed to happen in the lab. Block out time in your *University Matters Student Planner* for both the lab and the work you need to do before showing up at the lab.

- Clear up anything you don't understand about the lab well before it occurs. The TA, your fellow students or upper-year students will usually be happy to help you.
- The TA, and in some courses the professor, will supervise the lab and may or may not question you as you are performing the work—another good reason to bring your understanding up to a high level before the lab occurs.
- Often, the professor will provide an outline that shows you how the lab report is to be laid out (e.g., Introduction, Method & Materials, Results, Discussion). Follow it!

Some practical items:

- Make sure you know how long your report is supposed to be, especially if you think there may be an upper limit on how long it can be;
- If there are calculations required, show a sample calculation unless the TA specifically indicates it is superfluous;
- Make sure you present the data the professor is looking for, and that it is presented in the correct form. If the professor asks for a table, a graph likely won't suffice, even though they both present the same information;
- Present the data only once—if you provide a graph, there is no need to duplicate the information in a table, unless the professor calls for both;
- If your report includes a graph, table or figure, label it properly. The TA or professor will often specify a labelling approach. If none is specified, see if there are any posted directions or a posted marking scheme. You can discuss this with the TA, or ask upper-year students;
  - » Some labelling suggestions:
    - » Make sure the title is appropriately descriptive;
    - » For a graph, put proper labels on the axes, and the curves, bar charts, or whatever, that comprise the graph. Make sure the units of measurement are shown;
    - » For a table, label the rows and columns; indicate the units of measurement if not clear from the titles or the context;

- Although professors in most courses will encourage you to write in the active tense (e.g., I placed the chemical in a beaker) lab reports can be an exception. Some professors prefer to see them written in the passive tense (e.g., the chemical was placed in a beaker). Ask the TA if there is a preferred style;
- Cite your sources. Look for specification of a referencing style. Again, look for posted instructions, or ask your TA, upper-year students or your fellow students. Note that if you are being guided by the lab manual, it should be among the references you cite;
- In the discussion section of the report, make sure you show your knowledge of the underlying theory. Show how your findings support the theory. If the findings are contrary to theory, explain why this might have occurred. Explain any major assumptions that were made, and how they would account for differences between theoretical values, and actual obtained values;
- If you can, have a colleague read your lab report for clarity, punctuation and spelling;
- Get it in on time. Block out time to write up your report in your *University Matters Student Planner*.

8.6   Studying for tests, mid-terms and final exams

Listen carefully to any hints the professor may give in class to focus your studies.

Make a list of all the review tasks you wish to complete before your exam. Use the Exam/Test Study Worksheet in your *University Matters Student Planner* or download a copy from www.universitymatters.ca

Use your *University Matters Student Planner* to allocate time to each of the study tasks. Plan to finish your review with one clear day before the exam, during which you can do a complete overview in a relaxed manner. Since you are likely studying for more than one exam, you must be very disciplined with your time.
- Allow extra time for unforeseen eventualities. You may get a bad cold and be unable to study for a day or two. Make sure you are ahead of the game.

Review all of your class notes and any Web notes posted by the professor.
- Professors often spend class time on more important or difficult topics. Give them top priority.
- Some people absorb information best by writing out their notes several times. For example, you will have made notes in class, and then annotated

them shortly after class to make sure you understand them at a later date. As part of your exam study routine, you might want to make summary notes from your class notes. Summarize them again on 3" by 5" index cards and then study from the index cards. You can use different coloured cards for different courses, topics within a course, or types of information. For example, in a history course you could use white cards for names, facts and dates, and blue cards for major developments.

- If you are studying for a course in which different concepts build upon one another, make a flow chart that shows how this occurs. Put key explanatory information in the boxes of the flow chart to make a visual map of what you have learned from the course.
- It is much easier to remember material that you understand. Always make sure you understand the material before memorizing the points.
- If a lot of memory work is involved, divide the information into chunks and memorize each chunk; for example, memorize the contents of a particular index card. Mnemonics are acronyms or verses that are a powerful memory aid for some. Use them for lists of items you need to remember.

ROY-G-BIV
   The colours of the rainbow: red, orange, yellow, green, blue, indigo and violet.
HOMES
   The Great Lakes: Huron, Ontario, Michigan, Erie and Superior.
Sarah's Horse Must Eat Oats
   The Great Lakes in order of size: Superior, Huron, Michigan, Erie and Ontario.
See Mr. Huron Eating Oranges
   The Great Lakes in order from west to east: Superior, Michigan, Huron, Erie and Ontario.

You should already have done all of the assigned readings for the course. Go over them to see what you have highlighted, and review any notes you might have made in the margins.

- Reread your summary notes of chapters and assigned readings.
- Reread the more important or difficult chapters.

Review problems you previously completed and try some of the practice questions that are presented at the end of chapters, in study guides or on disks supplied with texts.

- Even if you don't complete all of the questions, scan them to see if you understand the direction they are taking. Ask yourself if you can see the solution approach. Can you identify the key points you would address?

Work with a classmate to quiz one another on course material. Have your classmate explain items you get wrong and do likewise for your classmate.
- Often getting a fresh explanation from your classmate leads to improved understanding for both of you. Explaining things to your classmate helps entrench concepts for you, and the repetition involved will help with recall later.

Ask the professor if old tests or exams are available on reserve in the library.
- Get them and do as many as you can;
- If there are too many problems to do by yourself, form a study group and share the workload. Set a date to meet again and exchange answers;
- Arrange for each group member to present to the group a problem or two for more difficult or important material.
- Sometimes the professor will give you a list of questions from which the exam essay topics will be selected. If you are not prohibited from working with others, form a study group to discuss all the key points that should be addressed in each question.

You may not have to prepare answers to all of the questions. For example, a professor might give you a list of 12 questions saying that seven of them will be on the exam and you will have to answer three of them.
- How many do you have to prepare?
  - » For the numbers folk, this is easy; for those who are numerically challenged, follow this logic:
  - » The professor will pick seven questions out of the 12. If you pick seven questions out of the 12, you might pick the five the professor did not pick, so you would only be prepared to answer two questions. Therefore, you need to pick one additional question. If you prepare answers to 8 questions that happen to include the five the professor did not pick, you will still be prepared to answer three questions.

- You might think that multiple-choice exams will be "easier," and be tempted to skim your text and notes hoping that the "aided recall" inherent in multiple-choice exams will see you through. This is unlikely. Most multiple-choice exams require that you understand the difference between a correct answer and an almost-correct answer, which can be challenging if you don't know the subject well enough. Pay particular attention to definitions or groups of ideas that are similar in meaning and be able to differentiate between them.

Make an effort to attend all tutorial sessions, especially those near the end of the year. The professor guides the teaching assistant with appropriate questions to supplement your learning.

Resist the urge to look at what is allegedly the exam or test if students claim to have a copy in their possession. Trust us when we say that it won't lead anywhere that is good for you.
- Don't hesitate to communicate with the professor if you become aware that a test has landed in the public domain;
- There have been cases in which the university required entire classes to rewrite exams because the test paper fell into unauthorized hands before the exam date.

Don't make travel plans before the final schedule for exams has been posted.
- Universities widely publicize the dates of the official exam period. The university rightfully acts as if it has a claim on your time up to the end of the exam period and will schedule accordingly. The schedule will not be changed to accommodate your flight home.

8.7   Writing exams

There is no substitute for a well-spent term for making
exams more bearable.

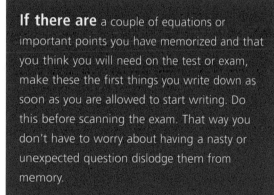

- Set the alarm clock and get a good
  night's sleep on the eve of each
  exam. On the morning of the
  exam, eat a healthy
  breakfast and avoid too
  much caffeine.
- Make sure you know
  what you will need to
  bring for the exam,
  such as a ruler, pen,
  pencils, eraser and
  calculator with fresh
  batteries, and also
  know what you are
  forbidden to bring into
  the exam hall. If you are
  not clear on this, ask
  your professor. Get
  everything together the
  night before so you are
  not scrambling to find
  things in the morning.
- Remember your Student
  ID card.
- Think positively. After all,
  the professor is only

If there are a couple of equations or important points you have memorized and that you think you will need on the test or exam, make these the first things you write down as soon as you are allowed to start writing. Do this before scanning the exam. That way you don't have to worry about having a nasty or unexpected question dislodge them from memory.

going to ask you things you are supposed to know, and that you will know if
you have followed a reasonable study protocol. Even if you haven't done as
much studying as you would have liked, there is nothing to be gained by
getting anxious. Focus on doing the best you can with what you know.

» Arrive ten minutes early;
» Stay focused to do your best;
» Take a couple of deep breaths to clear your mind and relax;
» Ignore the chatter of others around you;

» Try some relaxation techniques when you sit down. Close your eyes and shake the tension out of your arms. Relax your shoulders. Think of someone or something special.
- Read the exam instructions very carefully.
- Scan the exam and make sure you understand how many questions you are supposed to answer. Too many times, students answer all of the questions, when in fact they were supposed to choose from the questions offered. Look for wording such as: "Answer *three* of the following *five* questions."
- Determine your time allocation to the questions proportionate to marks. It's not a perfect system, but it's close enough. Often guidance is given in this regard.
- Complete the multiple-choice section of the exam first, keeping an eye on the time you have allocated to this section.
  » Read the question carefully. Underline any qualifying words such as "always," "often" and "never." Anticipate the answer before looking at the answer choices;
  » Read all of the answer choices carefully. Sometimes you will recognize many of the words but an additional word can make the seemingly obvious choice the wrong one;
  » Identify wrong answers from the multiple-choice alternatives and cross them out;
  » Make the best selection from the remaining options unless you are to be penalized for wrong answers. The exam instructions will state this clearly. In this case do not respond unless you are confident in your response. If there is no penalty, a guess is better than no answer;
  » Multiple-choice questions are usually made up of a line or two of preamble, and four or five alternative statements that follow from the preamble. If you are confused by a particular question, it can be effective to read the preamble and the complete phrase in the first possible answer, and then read the preamble again and the complete phrase from the second possible answer, and so on. You can try this at home with an old test to see if it helps you;
  » Don't look for patterns in responses. Multiple-choice questions are usually computer-bank generated, and the sequence of letter answers you observe as you go through the exam is meaningless. The fact that the answer has been D for the last five questions provides no information about whether or not the answer is D again for the next question;

Your three-hour exam could be structured as follows:

25 multiple-choice questions . . . . .worth 25 percent

Answer 3 of 4 short answer questions . . . . .worth 45 percent

Answer 1 of 3 essay topics . . . . .worth 30 percent

First, determine the number of minutes you have to allocate to the questions: 3 hours = 180 minutes. You can determine this before the exam starts since you will know the length of the exam. Then multiply the available number of minutes by the percentage of marks allocated to each section of questions.

Time to allocate to multiple choice . . . . .0.25 x 180 minutes = 45 minutes

(under 2 minutes per question)

Time to allocate to 3 short answers . . . . .0.45 x 180 minutes = 81 minutes

(27 minutes per question)

Time to allocate to 1 essay . . . . .0.30 x 180 minutes = 54 minutes

Suppose the exam starts at 2:00 p.m. Record at the beginning of each section of the exam the time by which you should start and finish each section:

Multiple-choice . . . . .Start 2:00 . . . . .Finish 2:45

Short answers . . . . .Start 2:45 . . . . .Finish 4:06

Essay . . . . .Start 4:06 . . . . .Finish 5:00

Since you have 45 minutes to answer 25 multiple-choice questions, you know

you have a little less than two minutes to spend on each question. Some questions you will answer quickly and others might take longer. If you are having difficulty with a question, circle it and come back to it once you have finished all of the multiple-choice questions as long you are within the time limit allocated to multiple-choice. If not, make a note at the end of the essay questions to "go back to multiple-choice." Then finish the rest of the exam, and if you have time, go back to the multiple-choice questions.

The few minutes spent planning the use of your time will alleviate any panic should you be concerned about how much time you have left to finish writing your exam. Sometimes the professor will be willing to tell you the exact structure of the exam beforehand. In these cases, map out your time allocations the night before the exam.

» Sometimes there is information in the multiple-choice answers that will be inadvertently helpful in the answering of an essay question elsewhere in the exam, or even in the answering of one of the other multiple choice questions;

» Sometimes the way an essay question is worded will inadvertently give you a clue to the answer to a multiple-choice question, or vice versa;

» If you haven't used all of the time you allocated to this section, go back and address the multiple-choice questions you passed over the first time through. If you are out of time, move on, but make a note at the end of the paper to go back to the multiple-choice questions later, even if only to pop in a couple of guesses if you are out of time.

Don't spend too long on one question. If you can't answer it, circle it clearly and come back to it. You will think better and be less panicky if you have answered all you can first. Erase the circle once you have answered the question;

- Read each short answer and essay question slowly several times and underline key words and each of the points that are to be addressed.

- Answer the "easiest" questions first, i.e., the questions you feel most able to answer well. This will help you feel more confident and reduce anxiety.

» Jot down the points you wish to cover in your answer before starting the response. This is where mnemonics and visual concept charts might come in handy;

» When you have finished your answer, reread the question to ensure you have addressed all aspects of the question;

» Proofread your answers; add any new thoughts that come to you, and correct any punctuation and spelling errors.

- If you have worked hard all term and feel well prepared, yet you still find a question on the exam that seems very unfamiliar, remember that professors seldom ask you questions that aren't answerable from the course material. They do, however, sometimes express things a little differently than you are used to.

» Tell yourself you do know the material, and that with a little "think time" the purpose of the question and the source of its answer will come to you;

» The source of the answer can surface while addressing another question on the exam paper. Your brain will keep working on the problem in the background.

- Part marks are the saviour of every student.
  - » If you don't know how to answer a question, put down whatever you do know. The more closely related this is to the question the better!
  - » If a particular feature of an exam problem prevents you from providing an answer, indicate this on the exam, and say what you would do but for this particular feature. Even putting down a general solution approach might get you some marks;
  - » If you are given a time warning and realize you will not be able to complete all of the questions, jot down the points you would have used to answer the questions and note that you ran out of time.
- Exam nerves can cause headaches, nausea, hot and cold sweats, a racing heart, fainting and other physical symptoms. If deep breathing and other relaxation techniques are not working for you, tell the invigilator right away. He or she may be able to help you. Afterwards, speak with Health Services for some more specific coping techniques.

> **If it's really** tough, just do the best you can do. Your peers are facing the same challenge.

9. Group Work

The experiences students have with group work tend to vary widely, from completely exasperating at the wrong end of the stick, to making friends for life at the other end. Think about the points set out below and see if you can grab the good end of the stick at the beginning of your university career, then hang on to it for dear life. Group work is a microcosm of real life.

9.1   Working with others

There are essentially three types of groups:
- Self-formed study groups;
- Self-formed project groups;
- Assigned project groups.

Group work is fun, challenging, rewarding and beneficial, but it can also be frustrating. It is important to remember that group work is assigned with good intent.
- You need to learn how to work with other people, and you are better off to practice and make all of your most grievous errors within the safe confines of a university course. It is not realistic to think you can avoid group work all

through university and then drop into a work setting and be proficient at it. Group work in the university environment offers you the chance to practice your skills when your job and salary are not on the line.

Usually study groups are not required but are a good idea. Be proactive and form a group early on, especially if you are an auditory learner. Refer to Chapter 6.3. You can exchange your class notes, discuss assigned readings, and perhaps even share textbooks and the responsibility of preparing chapter summaries and answers to practice questions. Quizzing each other before tests and exams is an efficient way to cover all of the material. Group meetings can be held in a relaxed, informal environment so blending some social interaction with your studies.

- Also, sometimes you can learn as much from your peers as from course material. Students have different opinions and thoughts to share with each other, which enhances the learning process. Your peers may use language and examples that you can relate to when clarifying points you do not understand.

University is a community of learning in that a student can learn as much from the other students as from the professors.
    Alan Harrison, Provost and Vice President, Academic, Carleton University

You will benefit from practicing important skills in group work:
- Oral communication of your ideas, your viewpoints, and your instructions;
- Listening skills;
- Taking direction from others;
- Sharing knowledge;
- Negotiation;
- The art of compromise;
- Taking on responsibility;
- Problem solving;
- Conflict resolution;
- Working with people from diverse backgrounds;
- Dealing with differing opinions;
- Relationship development;
- Earning the respect and trust of others.

Show your professor or teaching assistant the results of your group's work as soon as possible to see if you have correctly understood the assignment and are on the right track.

- On the other hand, don't go running to your professor every week! Once your direction is clear, be confident in your own decision-making ability.

9.2   Understanding your group members

Group work will lead you to discover that there are many different kinds of people with varying abilities. You can't change the natural tendencies of your group members, but you can assign roles to take advantage of their strengths or to help them improve certain skills.

Consider the following tendencies and abilities when assigning roles within the group:

- Leaders versus followers;
- Committed versus free rider;
- Consensus builders versus autocrats;
- Creative thinkers versus linear thinkers;
- Confident speakers versus shy presenters;
- Numbers-oriented versus artistically inclined.

You will discover that there are some truly selfish people and, fortunately, some truly wonderful people in the world, and you will gain the experience to tell one from the other.

9.3   Building an effective team

Setting things up from the start with a clear expectation of roles and responsibilities leads to team success.

Appoint a chairperson.

- This responsibility can rotate each meeting to give everyone a chance to practice this role or it can be assigned for the duration of the project to a person who particularly wishes to gain this experience.

- The chairperson should:
  - » Discuss the goals and objectives of the group. The goal is the end point, and the objectives are the steps that need to be completed along the way in order to achieve your goal;
  - » Discuss the work ethic and expectations from group members:
    - » Have each person describe his or her commitment level and build consensus as to the desired quality of the final product;
    - » Suggest to those members who fall outside of the majority that they find another group with like-minded participants;
    - » Determine the strengths of each group member and work with the group to assign work accordingly;
    - » Reach consensus within the group that slackers will not be carried. Refer to Chapter 9.4. Discuss consequences such as a peer review form that will be submitted with the final work if group members feel any members have significantly under-contributed;
  - » Keep the group focused on the issue at hand;
  - » Set deadlines to ensure the group makes progress at a reasonable pace;
  - » Ensure everyone gets a chance to put forward his or her thoughts;
  - » Encourage creative group problem solving where all ideas can be presented without criticism in order to develop insightful ideas and unique approaches;
  - » Avoid "group think." A sign of this is all members happily agreeing to the first suggestion;
  - » Summarize the main points;
  - » Keep meetings within the agreed-upon time limit;
  - » It is not the chairperson's job to chase people or make sure everything is done on time. Each person is responsible for being prepared for each meeting;

» Prepare or delegate responsibility for the preparation of an agenda for an upcoming meeting. After that meeting is over, prepare minutes to record what was delivered and summarize what was discussed, or agreed upon. Ideally the agenda should be e-mailed to group members before the meeting, and the minutes should be e-mailed no more than a day or two after the meeting.

Prepare effective agendas and minutes.

Agendas should specify:
- The time and place of the upcoming meeting;
- The discussion points for the upcoming meeting;
- A list of the deadlines or due dates that are on the horizon. If individuals are responsible for producing deliverables for the upcoming meeting, name them and the work you expect from them;
- Most of the time, the agenda should call for group members to provide an update at the meeting as to whether or not they are on track to meet their deadlines.

Minutes should:
- Summarize the key points discussed in the meeting;
- List any commitments that were made, show the group member's name and contact information, the task, and the due date;
  - » If there are any concerns with the level of a group member's commitment, the summary can be used to document what each member has done since the last meeting. This helps avoid misunderstandings and provides a record of each individual's progress, commitments, and performance against agreed due dates.
- Specify the time and place for the next meeting.

Meet regularly.
- If the project is a large one, you should insist on meeting at the same place and same time every week or at least every other week. A regular commitment improves attendance and motivates members to make progress and keep on track.
- Each member should come to meetings with additional topics and ideas to discuss, or e-mail them ahead of time to the person preparing the agenda.
- Each member should come to meetings prepared to offer suggestions, listen to others, encourage peers and admit mistakes.
- Socialize as a group occasionally. This will help you bond with each other and become more effective.

9.4   Slackers

Not all members will be equally
committed or capable.

- Focus on the effort of
  individuals as well as their
  output when assessing
  contributions. Remember, you
  are there to learn from your
  peers as well as help them develop
  skills.
- Some professors will allow you to
  shuffle group members, and others
  will insist you stay in groups once formed. Handle the challenge accordingly.
  Teamwork will be with you for the rest of your life, and you won't always be
  able to pick and choose the participants.
- Restate the work ethic and expectations within the group.
- Confront any slackers immediately.
- Don't waste time and energy trying to convert slackers who skip meetings or
  do not come prepared. Just document the facts in the minutes. Alert your
  professor if the problem is severe enough.
- If individual efforts are clearly unequal, propose to your professor your
  recommended mark allocation on a peer review form attached to your
  deliverable. It will carry more weight if all group members sign it to record
  their agreement with the allocation. However, the professor has the final
  decision as to how this will be handled.
- Take a positive attitude if you have to do more than your share of work. You
  will benefit in the long run.

10.   The Professor: An Integral Part
of the University Experience

We are frequently amazed at the gap in understanding between what professors are
there for and what students think professors are there for. The irony is that this misunderstanding occurs within one of the most important relationships students have
at university. You need to understand the role and responsibility of professors as
clearly as possible so you can make effective use of one of your most valuable
resources at university: your professors.

10.1 What is the professor's role and responsibility?

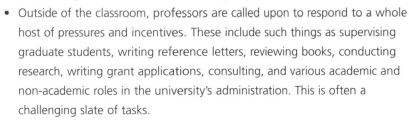

The professor's role is to achieve a reasonable balance among his or her teaching and other obligations.

- In the classroom and during posted office hours, all professors are there to deliver course content to you in a clear and interesting way.
- Outside of the classroom, professors are called upon to respond to a whole host of pressures and incentives. These include such things as supervising graduate students, writing reference letters, reviewing books, conducting research, writing grant applications, consulting, and various academic and non-academic roles in the university's administration. This is often a challenging slate of tasks.

10.2 How should I relate to my professor?

You should relate to your professor as if he or she were a very busy person. Assume that he or she has many pressing matters to deal with, and be as efficient as you can with his or her time.

- This reality may run counter to what you might think if you looked solely at hours allocated to the classroom. In many cases a professor will teach five or

80% Eighty percent of students report being satisfied with the quality of teaching they have experienced at their university.

88% Eighty-eight percent of students say that most of their professors are reasonably accessible outside of class to help students.

76% Seventy-six percent of students report that professors generally look out for students' interests.

60% Sixty percent of students indicate that some professors have taken a personal interest in their academic progress.[41]

41   Survey of Undergraduate University Students: University of Winnipeg, 2002, downloaded from http://www.uwinnipeg.ca/index/cms-filesystem-action?file=pdfs/future/cusc.pdf on April 6, 2005.

fewer half-courses in an entire year. A focus on classroom hours misses the hours of preparation for lectures, including time devoted to the creation of assignments, tutorial lessons, tests and exams, and the time spent with individual students and teaching assistants.

- This reality may run counter to what you observe when you see professors in their offices or the hallways. They often dress informally, and casual observation gives the impression they tend to poke around with their computers, talk on the telephone, or chat with people. Casual observation misses the many deadlines professors face with respect to each of their commitments.

- If the professor is willing to let you pick up something from his or her office, pick it up and run. Admittance to a professor's office is not licence to hang around and discuss whatever it is you just picked up, least of all the professor's approach to marking a test or paper. Walk out and leaf through it on your time, not the professor's.

- If you have interrupted a professor in his or her office to ask a question, thank the professor upon obtaining the answer and leave promptly. Do not use the opportunity to engage the professor in chit-chat unless the professor signals his or her interest by asking you a question.

- Respect the professor's office hours and keep questions specific.

- Seek guidance but take the initiative. You do not need to clear every activity with your professor. You must take responsibility for your own ideas and progress.

- If you disagree with your professor, state your objections or concerns clearly and calmly. If you feel something about your relationship is not working well, discuss it with him or her. Whenever possible, suggest steps the professor could take to address your concerns.

Always communicate with your professor in an open-door setting. This helps protect both the student and the professor from harassment allegations. This advice holds true for same gender interactions.

If you are a serious student, and treat your professor with respect, you may be able to build a meaningful relationship that will last into the years ahead. Professors take great delight in seeing their students succeed.

- Professors are happy to help committed students by providing letters of reference to potential employers or to support graduate school applications.

From day one, I would encourage you to get to know your professors and to start building professional relationships with them. When you enter university, professors may seem intimidating, but after you get over the fear, you realize there is a lot to learn from them, both in and out of the classroom. I have asked for their advice about coursework, summer jobs and graduate programs. In addition to being generally interesting people, and great allies during university, they can be very helpful later on in life, whether or not you decide to further your education. I applied to more than a dozen universities after I graduated from Carleton and each school's application required two to three reference letters, which ended up being a lot of letters, especially when you consider that the professor has to tailor-make the letters to meet the unique requirements of each institution. The application process was gruelling, but knowing that I had the support of professors from my undergraduate program made things easier. I was able to find professors who were willing to make the time commitment required to help me out. I am confident they did so because they remembered me as someone who had earned their support. Their support in every aspect of my career thus far has helped me obtain a place at The Paul H. Nitze School of Advanced International Studies at Johns Hopkins University, in Washington D.C., and for this, I thank them.

Aliya, Carleton University. Commerce '03

- Many professors are a valuable source of contacts when you are job hunting. Remember, though, their time is precious and they will only be available to help those students who have worked hard.

The relationships I built with my professors proved extremely valuable, especially in career planning. One professor not only took the time to discuss various options with me, but also introduced me to professionals in the finance industry. As a result, I was able to secure a corporate finance position in Toronto with one of the big five banks.

Matt, Carleton University, International Business '04

There are some realities about typical professors that you should be aware of:
- Most are highly intelligent and have a track record of hard work and success both inside and outside of university environments;
- Some are also successful professionals such as lawyers, public accountants or physicians. They understand and expect hard work. They have worked for what they have. As you might expect, they will have a hard time with

students who do not appear to work hard or do not appear to be dedicated to their studies. They will very likely have a difficult time with students who appear to "want something for nothing."

10.3 Professors don't want to...

hear:

- "What do I need to do to get an A?"
  - » Work hard, attend class, ask intelligent questions and learn at least 90 percent of the material cold!
- "Do I have to buy the text?"
  - » Yes, why else was it specified?
- "Do I have to read all of the assigned chapters for the exam?"
  - » Yes, unless otherwise instructed.
- "There was nothing from that chapter on the exam, so we wasted our time reading it."
  - » You are responsible for learning all of the assigned material in each course. Tests are there to help you gauge how successful your learning has been.
- Poor excuses..."my bus was late"..."my pet ferret ate my paper"..."Aunt Mildred was ill"..."Aunt Mildred died" (again?)..."My flight back from the Bahamas gets back two days after reading week finishes"...

see:

- Students sitting in class wearing headphones, reading the newspaper, chatting, Internet surfing, dozing or any combination thereof.

receive:

- E-mails seeking clarification on administrative matters that you missed because you wandered into class late.
- E-mails based on the "e-mail shorthand" you use with your friends on MSN. An e-mail to your professor should be clear, concise, and free from spelling or grammatical errors. Anything less signals laziness, stupidity, disrespect, or all of the foregoing. The following are sad but true examples!
  - » "Well I'm kinda lost, I'm not sure how to study for this final. What would you suggest? I wanna do well. I really want to get an A. Please help."
  - » "I'm just wundring are we gonna start the tutorial this Friday?"
  - » "Hey prof, can u list out the differences between edition 1 and 2 of the text?"

> I wish I had understood sooner the importance of creating relationships with my professors. In my experience, questions were better answered, topics better understood, and more opportunities were afforded to me when I bothered to get to know a professor and have them know me. Talk to your professors! You do not have to be a suck-up, but a professor that better understands you and your goals is that much more able to help you out.
>
> Katrina, University of Toronto, Art History '04

10.4 Professors do want to...

hear:

- "How can I make sure I get the most out of this course?"
- "How can I improve my final mark, given my marks to date?"
- The truth. Admit if you are not able to answer questions in class due to lack of preparation. Apologize and say you will be better prepared next class. Then be prepared!

see:

- Students who are alert, receptive and engaged:
  » Professors want their students to enjoy learning and to succeed. They know that some students will be more interested than others, and can tolerate quite a bit of variation. However, you owe the professor and your classmates respectful behaviour in class.

receive:

- Serious, polite requests by e-mail:
  » "I am studying for the final and I was wondering if you could give me some additional guidance. If possible, could you tell me if there will be any calculations required in the multiple-choice questions? Also, would you suggest focusing more on certain lectures as opposed to others? Chapters 3 and 7 seem to contain the key material. Thanks."
- Requests that show you have taken the initiative to find the information elsewhere first.
  » Before visiting your professor or sending any e-mails, check your course outlines for comments on the format of tests and exams;

» Check your notes and confirm with your fellow students whether any tips were given in class. Professors are happy to expand on what they have said, but if it is obvious you were not paying attention or skipped class you may not receive much support.

11. So Now You Have to Cope

If you have read *University Matters* up to here, you have been bombarded with a lot of useful suggestions. But nothing works all of the time. Your job as a student is not to live a problem-free life. Your job is to greet problems with resolve, dignity and, yes, even skill. Your job is to be proud of yourself that you did so, whether you ultimately succeed, or not.

Many people have difficulty asking for help. Seeking help is a sign of maturity. Very few people are proficient at everything. Let others help you improve in areas where life is challenging for you. You can return the favour to someone else one day.

11.1   Things can go wrong

Sometimes things don't work out the way we would like. This is sometimes due to bad luck and sometimes due to bad management. Whatever the source, coping with adverse outcomes is a useful skill for university, and for all of life.

Most people strike a balance between pushing the boundaries and accepting the associated risks, versus staying within a comfort zone. Failure is just one of the signs that you have pushed the boundary.

We should not be too hard on ourselves for a bad outcome. Only those who live within their capabilities by a wide margin go through life with little or no failure. Is this what you want? Probably not!

11.2   Illness

If you are ill and do not feel able to write a test or exam, or submit work on time, you should go to a doctor while you are still sick and request a medical note. Submit the doctor's note to your professor.

• Send a brief e-mail indicating you will not be writing an exam or will be missing a deadline. This is polite and helps the professor account for missing work.

- You need not tell your professor the nature of your illness. The medical note will suffice.
- As soon as you are able, contact your professor to discuss how he or she wants to handle whatever you have missed. Often the course outline will spell this out.

11.3   Persevere

If you do poorly on an assignment, paper or exam, try not to let a critique of your work get you down. This is especially hard if you made a serious effort and had expected a better mark. You must look at these situations as learning experiences and opportunities to improve. Remember, the feedback is about how you approached the assignment and not about you as a person.

Learning from your mistakes is essential. Many a student has commented, "It never fails. The question I got wrong on the assignment was on the exam." Take the time to figure out the correct answer when the material is fresh in your mind.

- Make sure you understand where you went wrong.
  - » If it is not clear to you where you went wrong, ask your professor or TA for more detailed feedback. Make sure the professor or TA understands that this is not a negotiation for marks, but rather a discussion about learning what you can do to improve for the next time.

Lesson in perseverance: Abraham Lincoln[42]

His mother died in his childhood. The lady he loved and was engaged to marry also died. When his grocery business went bankrupt, he worked for seventeen years to pay back his creditors. He tried politics and was defeated by his opponents many times. He struggled to achieve noble aspirations and often was depressed by the struggle, but he persevered with dignity and patience.

1831 – Failed in business	1843 – Defeated for Congress
1832 – Defeated by legislature	1855 – Defeated for Senate
1833 – Again failed in business	1856 – Defeated for Vice-President
1835 – Sweetheart died	1858 – Defeated for Senate
1836 – Suffered nervous breakdown	1860 – Elected President of the U.S.
1838 – Defeated for speaker	

---

42   Downloaded from www.geocities.com/joelshiver/quotes.html, April 16, 2005.

- If you think the mark assigned to your work is unfair, you can ask your professor to regrade your work. If your professor doesn't think there are grounds to improve the mark, you may have the right to request that someone else regrade your work. The university may charge you a fee for this service, and sometimes it is refundable if more marks are awarded. There is also the possibility that your mark could be reduced rather than increased.

- Few professors will allow supplementary work to improve a poor mark, but if you ask politely, you might find out otherwise. Try explaining to your professor where you went wrong and ask for an opportunity to improve your mark by resubmitting a supplementary paper.

- Think back to childhood as you learned to tie shoelaces, skate or catch a ball. Or think of the first time you hit the slopes on your snowboard. Persistence will pay off!

11.4 Help is available

Use the university resources. The support structure is there; all you have to do is reach out and use it.

- Universities are in the teaching and learning business. They are seriously committed to supporting students who are not coping well. Seek guidance from Academic Services to determine how best to get back on track.
- Ask Student Services if an upper-year student is available to act as your mentor.
- You are not alone with your challenges and queries. Many others deal with the same issues and concerns. Talking with others who have challenges can motivate you to work out a plan together to get back on track.
- Hard work compensates for a multitude of sins at university.
  » If you feel you have fallen behind, make a detailed schedule of all that you have to do to catch up on your work. Then do it!

- » Use any uncommitted time in your schedule to do work that you have neglected to date;
- » Put all social commitments on the back burner;
- » While catching up is difficult, you can make progress, maybe even enough to convert a "failing" situation into a "passing" one.
- Approach the professor for support.
  - » Explain the situation honestly;
  - » Present your proposal to remedy the problem;
  - » Request the professor's support and any time extensions that you require. If you do get an extension, do your absolute best to live by your new deal.
- Seek input from other students in the class who have done well.
  - » Fellow students are usually willing to provide guidance to those who are seriously trying to improve. Make it clear you are seeking guidance and helpful tips rather than an easy ride.
- Consider dropping a course if you feel overwhelmed. Consult with an academic advisor, and refer to Chapter 4.3 to ensure you understand the potential implications. You may be able to take a summer course to compensate. It is often possible take a course at a different university, perhaps even over the Internet, that will count toward your program. The academic advisor can help you with this as well. Refer to Chapter 4.3.

11.5 Changing direction

You may have arrived at university feeling certain you had your program, major and career figured out. Some people know from an early age what they want to do and stick with it. Others figure it out as they broaden their horizons and are exposed to new experiences.

- Some students change their majors after the end of their first year. For many, all or most of the courses they took in first year will count toward their new program, so the change will have no effect on their year of graduation.
- Some students drop out of university because they realize they do not wish to pursue their chosen field of study; others do so because they feel

- Fifteen percent of young Canadians attending college or university leave within two years. Of those, 41 percent reported they didn't like their program or felt that it wasn't for them and 11 percent cited lack of money.
- Thirty-eight percent of those who left returned within two years.[43]

---

43   c. f. Who pursues postsecondary education, who leaves and why: Results from the Youth in Transition Survey. Statistics Canada, Catalogue no. 81-595-MIE – No. 026.

overwhelmed by the myriad of challenges they are juggling; some realize they would prefer a field of study that leads to a specific job and, therefore, explore vocational programs at colleges.

- Don't panic and make a rash decision!
  - » Figuring out what you want to do with your life is a big part of the learning process and is one of the reasons you are at university;
  - » Use the resources outlined in Chapter 11.4 and speak to professors who teach in other programs for support and redirection;
  - » Spending an extra year switching programs is much better than completing a degree in a field you don't enjoy. Consider yourself lucky to realize and confront this now, rather than five years into a career you don't enjoy;
  - » If you are finding it difficult to be living far from home, consider moving to a university closer to home, where you will have more family support;
  - » You may worry that your parents will be disappointed. It is more likely they will respect your maturity and ability to make your own decisions. If they express disappointment, you may have been following their dreams and ambitions rather than yours.

NOTES

NOTES

Life Skills

Life Skills

When you arrive at university, there will be a notable lack of intervention in your life by parents, teachers and other adults. You won't likely hear anyone telling you things like:

- Do your homework;
- Go to bed;
- Take out the garbage;
- Do your laundry;
- Study for your test;
- Start your assignment;
- Have a healthy breakfast;
- Get some fresh air.

This gives the illusion that the restrictions you were so aware of in your final months of high school don't apply anymore. Nothing could be further from the truth. There is no difference in the restrictions you are facing. What is different is the way they manifest themselves. At home, a poor decision might bring with it parental intervention, and a resulting change in your behaviour. At university, there won't be parental intervention. In fact, it is likely that no one will care that much what you are doing or not doing. You can do what you want without interference, but you have to live with the consequences. It's up to you to consider the various behaviours available to you and the related consequences, and to adopt one behaviour over the alternatives because you prefer the consequences of that behaviour. In this section we provide material that will help you link behaviours to consequences, and to make good decisions.

Biggest Challenges

- Resisting the urge to hang out with friends rather than studying
- Establishing a regular sleeping schedule
- Choosing nutritious foods
- Using street drugs
- Overuse of alcohol
- Sticking to your budget
- Getting along with roommates
- Exiting unhealthy relationships
- Seeking help from others

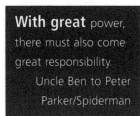

With great power, there must also come great responsibility.
Uncle Ben to Peter Parker/Spiderman

12. Your Social Life

Your social life will take up a lot of your time at university. Make it worthwhile for you by thinking things through a little bit. But most importantly, have fun! Benefit from the warmth and support of friendships, many of which will last a lifetime. Also, remember to extend a welcoming hand to those around you.

12.1 Friendships

Choose your friends wisely. Think about who you wish to spend time with and why. We tend to form closer bonds with people who have similar values.

- Good friends will always be considerate of your feelings and help you feel good about yourself. They are affirming, empowering and supportive. Nurture these relationships.
- People who are selfish, mean or unfair are not your friends, no matter how outgoing, connected or funny they are. You deserve better. Politely but firmly distance yourself.
- In friendships, actions speak louder than words. Think about the actual behaviours of your friends. Saying nice things but behaving badly does not amount to a friendship. Again, politely but firmly distance yourself.
- Good friends will support your need to study if you indicate it is a priority.
- Sometimes it is fun to hang out with "party animals." Just be sure you are in control of your time and that you don't get swayed to spend more time partying than your schedule will allow.
- You can meet new friends many different ways:
  - » In classes and tutorials

- » Through clubs and associations
- » By volunteering
- » In athletics groups
- » In study groups
- » In the campus lounge
- » Via other friends
- » Socializing in the campus pubs
- » At sporting events
- You will not meet new people sitting in front of the TV or computer playing games. Get out and get involved.
- Most of us fear rejection and sometimes balk at introducing ourselves to people we don't know. Recognize that the person you are thinking of talking to probably shares this fear, so:
  - » Walk up and introduce yourself. It is easier to do if you select someone who is standing alone. Avoid pairs, as they are often engaged in conversation;
  - » If you need practice, try this out on a few people before approaching that very important classmate you have been dying to meet;
  - » If you don't get a warm welcome, be ready with, "I am sorry, I seem to have caught you at a bad time. Nice meeting you." A lot of the time, the bad reaction has more to do with some other event in their day rather than your approach, so try to be forgiving. Also, only the hardest of hearts will fail to recognize and respect a classy response to an awkward situation of their own making.
- Remember his or her name. To do this, say the name of the person out loud as soon as you can. For example, if the person says, "I'm Frank," you can say,

"Nice to meet you Frank, I'm Nancy." Try to work the person's name into the conversation within a few minutes.

» If you aren't good at this, do a bit of thinking about it in advance, perhaps on one of your walks to and from campus. You can even rehearse some lines out loud in private, or if you like, with someone else equally unsure of this process. It's worth working on; it's an important lifetime skill;

If you forget the person's name, deal with it right away. Most people are very forgiving if you say, "Sorry, I can't believe that your name just slipped my mind." Or, "I am sorry, I've been reading for three hours straight and my mind just went blank. Can you tell me your name again?" Most people will be glad to repeat it, and you might be surprised by how many times your counterpart says, "And your name again...?"

• Think up a few opening lines. Open-ended questions work best; that is, anything that can't be answered with a simple yes or no, or a fact. Be ready to counter a one-word response with, "Oh really, why do you think that?"
  » Resist using the same line with different people so that your approach appears genuine rather than contrived;
  » Think up some interesting answers to the likely questions you will get when you chat with someone new, another good use of walking time. If asked your field of study, it is better to say, "I am studying some really interesting issues in..." rather than grunting out, "Politics." You may get back, "Oh really, like what?" and then you are off and running;
  » If you feel you need practice with this, note that anyone around you is a good target. Try it with a clerk at the store, if they don't appear too busy, or a taxi driver, or a person standing in a line with you.
• Be a good listener, which will encourage the other person to talk about himself or herself. Inquire about his or her interests.
• If someone else walks up, introduce the other person.
• Don't be a shoulder gazer. It is never polite to be looking over a person's shoulder for someone more interesting to talk to. Even though you think you are being subtle, this behaviour is almost always very obvious to your conversation partner.
• Maintain contact with the people you meet. Say hi if you see them again, shoot them an e-mail, or send them things you come across that you think might interest them. You do not need to be "best friends" with everybody, but fellow students may be very helpful one day for a whole host of reasons.

- Friends often have opinions that are different from yours, and this can lead to disagreements. This can take you by surprise, is almost always upsetting, and can negatively affect your focus on studying.
  - » Talk the situation over as soon as you have calmed down. Try to resolve the conflict with the person involved rather than by turning to another friend. Gossip travels really quickly on campus and can ruin friendships for life;
  - » Use "I feel frustrated..." rather than "You make me feel frustrated...";
  - » Be the first one to say sorry, at least some of the time;
  - » If you can't come to terms, then "agree to disagree" and accept that you have differing views or ways of handling situations. Try to see the situation from your friend's perspective. It is often possible to respect another person and their point of view, even though you do not share it.
- Don't hold grudges. Harbouring your own feelings of anger and resentment is very hard on you and your emotional well-being. It makes it difficult to see all that is positive around you and gets in the way of your enjoyment of life. Be kind to yourself by letting go of these feelings, and moving on. Forgiving someone does not mean you have to approve of what they did, nor does it mean you ever have to talk to them again. Forgiveness is about recognizing another's point of view, and another's human failings that may have led to their offending behaviour. That is all.
- Read about the Myers-Briggs Type Indicator, which categorizes personality based on an individual's preferred way of thinking and behaving. The Myers-Briggs approach will help you understand why some of the behaviours you observe seem so different from your own. Ask the psychology department if any graduate students are administering the test and offer to participate. For a discussion, see the following Web site: www.psychometrics.com/tests/DetailsPage.cfm?ID=50&testcode=TES001
- Stay true to your values and avoid blindly following the crowd. Take pride in your choices and decisions.
- Help others, but if a friend has a serious problem, encourage him or her to get professional help from Student Services. When you are not equipped to help someone, you might become overwhelmed by his or her problems. Refer to Chapter 16.

"Life" and university do not necessarily mix well. Crises with friends and family can really take a toll on your work. It is essential to learn to keep them as separate as possible.

Katrina, University of Toronto, Art History '04

12.2 Balance

A key challenge for you will be juggling the many opportunities to interact with other students while sticking to your planned study schedule. It is a challenge for most students.

- Friends may not mean to tempt you away from your work, but given everyone's different schedules and study habits, many friends will want to relax when you had planned to study.
- Get your work done and build in some time for fun later in the evening.
- Time to relax and laugh with your friends is important for your emotional well-being.
- On the other hand, there will be very busy points during the term when you just have to put your nose to the grindstone with the promise to yourself that you'll have lots of fun once you have met the academic demands at hand.
- You will have more fun socializing if your studies are under control.
- Benchmark yourself against students you respect. If you seem to be the only one always able to go to the pub, think again. If you are the only one always working, revisit your approach to time management, talk with Academic Services about your study habits, or discuss your approach with a friend you respect.
- A little bit of solo time is healthy too. You need some personal reflection time, so try not to spend every non-studying minute hanging around with friends. Take some time to go for a walk by yourself or write some e-mails to family and friends you haven't contacted in a while.

12.3 Try something new

University life offers you the chance to push the boundaries by trying many new activities and exploring different views and ways of thinking.

- The perspective you gain from this can be very powerful in helping you understand and solidify your own thoughts and opinions for your life ahead.
- Take advantage of opportunities to increase your understanding and tolerance of points of view that are different from your own.

- Investigate the different clubs and associations on campus that will enable you to:
  » Explore alternate philosophical approaches to life;
  » Investigate different religious beliefs;
  » Discuss political ideologies different from your own;
  » Talk to people with backgrounds different from your own;
  » Explore and participate in different cultural activities;
  » Try new activities in such areas as drama, debating, fencing, music lessons or learning to play a new musical instrument.

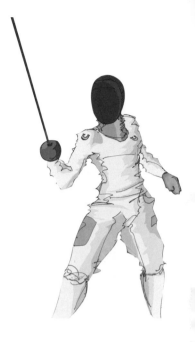

University is about a lot more than academics. The person you go in as is very different from the person who graduates.

Jeff, University of Toronto, Geography '06

13. Nurturing Your Mind, Body and Soul

Despite all the discussion of particular skills in the preceding chapters, we have yet to address a very important partner of yours: your physical and emotional health. You need to be healthy. Everything good will seem better if you are, and almost everything bad will seem worse if you aren't. Invest in your physical and emotional health bit by bit over the long haul and it will pay off for you.

13.1 Sleep

Your brain and body need to be well-rested to think clearly and perform well in all aspects of life.

- Everyone is unique when it comes to sleep, but seven to eight hours per night is the common recommendation.
- It is pretty hard to change your natural sleep requirements into something else, so be realistic about what your body is telling you.

- Keep to a regular schedule in accordance with your body clock. Fifty-five hours of sleep a week doesn't count if it is two days with no sleep and then eleven hours a day for the rest of the week.
- If you have trouble sleeping, avoid stimulating activities, late-night thrillers, too much alcohol, and caffeine after lunchtime.
- Avoid consuming caffeine at night when studying. Caffeine may help you stay awake to study, but you won't get a good night's sleep. You will not perform well the next day if you have not slept well or are exhausted from an all-nighter.
- Exercise daily but try to avoid the four-hour period before going to bed.
- Alcohol interferes with sleep. You may pass out easily when your head hits the pillow, but you will likely have an interrupted sleep, which will impair your productivity the next day.
- Information learned during the day is transferred from short-term memory to long-term memory during sleep. A poor night's sleep will interfere with this process and lessen your ability to learn and remember.
- Try hot milk or chamomile tea in the evening. They both have properties that help you sleep.
- If you have trouble waking up, arrange for a friend to telephone you, or knock on your door in the morning.
- If you have trouble getting out of bed, try establishing regular hours for sleeping and getting up. Adhering to a sensible bedtime ensures you will be well-rested, and ready to awaken and get going at the predetermined time in the morning.

13.2 Avoid the frosh fifteen

The frosh fifteen refers to the observation that many students gain fifteen pounds during their first year away at university. This is not a myth![44]

---

44 c.f. Conway-Smith, W., For most students, the weight gain is real, *The Ottawa Citizen*, May 3, 2004, page A10.

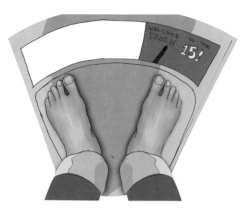

- One pound of weight is gained by consuming 3,500 calories more than your body requires. If you consume 150 calories per day more than you need, you will consume an additional 54,750 calories in a year, resulting in a weight gain of 15.6 pounds. One beer is 150 calories, a chocolate bar is 250 calories, a muffin is 300 calories, a slice of pizza is 250 calories, fancy coffees can be upwards of 400 calories, and burgers and fries soar up to 1,000 calories.

- You will gain weight if you make poor eating choices, drink too much beer, and settle into a sedentary lifestyle lounging around with friends.

- Be aware of your eating habits. Do you reach for unhealthy comfort foods when you are studying or lonely? Keep only healthy snacks on hand. A chocolate bar or a couple of cookies once in a while won't hurt you, but calories add up fast if eaten on a daily basis.

- Stick to a regular eating schedule and make the time to prepare food or you will eat too much processed food which is often high in fat and salt; it can make you gain weight and feel lethargic.

- If you are on a meal plan and eat at the campus cafeteria, survey the options and choose the healthy ones. Vegetable stir-fries, pitas, the salad bar, chicken and fish are tasty and low in fat.

- Minimize the starch options by selecting only one of rice, pasta, potatoes or bread. Even better, ask for a double serving of vegetables and skip the "starch" option altogether.

- Finish your meal before surveying the desserts. Treat yourself occasionally to your favourite dessert, but don't make it a daily habit.

- Avoid the temptation to eat high-fat, greasy food late at night after partying. Drink lots of water instead.

- If an all-you-can-eat buffet is available to you, limit how often you use it.

- Nobody is perfect, so be happy if it's the frosh five!

Eat properly, exercise regularly, and if you choose to drink alcohol, do so in moderation.

13.3 Make nutritious choices

Plan nutritionally balanced meals. Stick Canada's Food Guide to Healthy Eating onto your fridge to remind you to make healthy food choices a daily habit. www.hc-sc.gc.ca/hpfb-dgpsa/onpp-bppn/food_guide_rainbow_e.html

Eating a well-balanced diet is the best way to obtain the vitamins, minerals and dietary fibre you require for a healthy body and mind.

- Make it a habit to check the labels of boxes and cans to ensure you are getting enough vitamins and minerals while minimizing saturated fats, trans fats, cholesterol and sodium intake.
- Vitamins B and C are water soluble and eliminated in urine; they need replenishing daily. Vitamins A, D, E and K are fat-soluble and stored in our bodies.
- Consult with your doctor to discuss vitamin supplements if you are a vegetarian or eat a narrow selection of foods.
- See Appendix 2—Nutrition: the Good and the Bad.
- Post our Vitamins and Minerals Checklist on your fridge. A copy is in your *University Matters Student Planner* or download a copy from www.universitymatters.ca
- Some excellent reference books include:
  - » *Eat, Drink, and Be Healthy: The Harvard Medical School Guide to Healthy Eating* by Walter C. Willett and P. J. Skerrett (ISBN 0743223225);
  - » *The Enlightened Eater: A Guide to Well-Being Through Nutrition* by Marion Kane and Rosie Schwartz (ISBN 045880780X);
  - » *Leslie Beck's 10 Steps to Healthy Eating* by, you guessed it, Leslie Beck (ISBN 0143016024);

Trans fats are bad fats that contribute to heart disease. You should minimize your trans fat intake. See Appendix 2 for more details. Some products identify their trans fat content on the nutritional information panel that appears on their packaging. Many don't, but it is easy to calculate. First add up the quantities of polyunsaturates, monounsaturates and saturates reported on the panel. If this equals the total fat content, also reported on the panel, the product contains a negligible amount of trans fats or none at all. Any difference between the reported total fat amount and the sum of the items mentioned above is the trans fat content of the product.

- » *Thin for Life: 10 Keys to Success from People Who Have Lost Weight and Kept It Off* by Anne M. Fletcher (ISBN 0618340556).
- For more nutrition tips check this Web site: www.dieticians.ca
- Always eat a nutritious breakfast to get a protein, calcium and low-fat boost. This is the meal that fuels your body for the start of a productive day. Your brain needs this food to function optimally. You need this food to focus, concentrate and study.
  - » If you skip breakfast, you will probably end up being so hungry by mid-morning that you will head to the coffee shop, grab a high-fat, high-sugar snack, and end up hungry again shortly thereafter.
- Eat at regular times during the day. It is better to eat a moderate amount five times per day at roughly the same times every day than to eat a lot only once or twice per day.
- Choose fresh foods as often as you can to minimize trans fats, sodium and chemicals.
- Keep hydrated with plenty of water, which will keep you alert. Dehydration can cause lethargy and headaches. It is a common error to eat when your body is thirsty rather than hungry.
- If you are on a meal plan at the cafeteria, ensure you make healthy choices. Strive for five to ten fruit and vegetable servings every day, and treat yourself to high-fat choices only occasionally. Refer to the following Web site for additional suggestions to increase your fruit and vegetable intake: www.5to10aday.com
- When you are studying you need to snack regularly to keep your energy level up. If you have chips in your room you will eat them. Avoid this temptation by keeping healthy snacks on hand, such as:
  - » Low-fat yogourt;
  - » Your favourite fresh fruits, especially whatever is in season;
  - » Sliced apple with cheese or peanut butter.

> **Make a healthy** lunch instead of grabbing fast food when you are hungry. You will eat better and save money.

> **Thirty-six percent** of students using food services on campus report being dissatisfied or very dissatisfied.[45]

An apple a day keeps the doctor away. Apples have about 90 calories, are full of nutrients and fibre, and help keep blood sugar steady.

---

45   Survey of Undergraduate University Students: University of Winnipeg, 2002, downloaded from http://www.uwinnipeg.ca/index/cms-filesystem-action?file=pdfs/future/cusc.pdf on April 6, 2005.

- » Fresh fruit smoothies made with low-fat yogourt;
- » Prewashed, cut-up fresh vegetables, such as carrots, peppers and celery with hummus or salsa;
- » Whole-wheat pita with hummus or salsa;
- » Small servings of nuts: almonds, cashews, peanuts, sunflower seeds or trail mix;
- » Pretzels;
- » High-fibre, whole-grain crackers with no trans fats (free of hydrogenated oils) together with low-fat cheese;
- » Your favourite high-fibre, low-sugar cereal;
- » Instant hot cereal;
- » Canned sardines;
- » Nachos with microwaved low-fat cheese;
- » Raisins;
- » Cheerios or another low-fat cereal;
- » Low-fat granola bars;
- » Fig Newtons;
- » Fruit and veggie bars;
- » Skim milk;
- » Hot chocolate made with skim milk;
- » Whole-wheat bagel with low-fat cream cheese;
- » Twizzlers.

> **The best way** to minimize your junk-food intake is to make sure it doesn't get into your house in the first place. Remember that all the calories that come across your doorstep have to go somewhere.

- If you don't have something healthy on hand, take a short break and walk to a store to pick up something nutritious. You will get the added benefit of exercise, fresh air and sunlight.
- Minimize sugar boosts from chocolate bars and high-fat pastries since your concentration and alertness will "crash" shortly thereafter.
- Keep low- or zero-calorie fluids handy all the time. Water and herbal teas will boost your fluid intake and don't add calories.
- Always put your snack on a plate or in a bowl. It is too easy to overeat if you munch out of the box.
- Avoid keeping junk food in your room and resist picking up the following:
  - » Chocolate bars, chips, donuts, and other high-fat junk food;
  - » Commercially prepared muffins;
  - » Full-sugar soft drinks, which contain an average of nine teaspoons of sugar in each can.
- Speak to a doctor in Health Services if you wish to initiate a weight-loss program. An unsupervised diet during the school term may leave you low in

energy. Be wary of the latest "fad" diets. A doctor can help you lose weight by referring you to a nutritionist or suggesting an exercise plan and a healthy shift in your eating habits. You can also get a referral to a dietician in private practice by calling 1-888-901-7776.

13.4   Alcohol

Do not drink and drive. Ever. Be a good friend and prevent others from driving if they are impaired. Car accidents can kill the driver, passengers and innocent others.

If you have had a few drinks, you may think you are "feeling fine." But it is certain that your reactions are slower, and your focus less sharp. Remember that other drivers may have been drinking, and you have to be extra alert and on the defensive to protect yourself from them.

Although the number of times per week that students drink is not particularly high, the amount they drink at one time is a significant concern. 62.7 percent of students reported five or more drinks on a single occasion and 34.8 percent reported drinking eight or more drinks on a single occasion.[46]

If you choose to drink, do so in moderation, bearing in mind your obligations for the next day.

- A hangover completely wipes out your productivity the next day. You can have fun without getting loaded. You are out with friends to laugh and meet people, not to waste money and wake up feeling rotten. The key is moderation.
- Some people drink to escape their troubles, or drown their sorrows. You are much better off to treat a friend to pizza and talk out your worries.
- If you are going out in a group, agree upon a designated driver. Rotate this responsibility the next time out.
- Be proactive and promote responsible drinking. You can obtain posters targeting university students from Mothers Against Drunk Driving (MADD) Canada, www.madd.ca

46   First National Study of Drug Use Among University Students Released by the Centre for Addiction and Mental Health. Based on data gathered from 7800 undergraduate students in 16 universities across Canada.

- Record in writing how you feel "the morning after" an evening when you have overindulged.
  » Post your feelings and thoughts where you can read them before your next social outing;
  » Many people, young and old, laugh or brag about how bad they felt after a night of overindulgence. It is not cool to damage your body and wipe out a day that you could have enjoyed.

- Make it a habit to drink soft drinks or alternate one alcoholic drink with water or a soft drink. This is a good lifetime habit. You will feel better, your long-term health prospects will be improved, and you will spend less money!
- Notice the impact on your wallet of a night at the bar.
- Alcohol and beer contribute empty calories, that is, calories that contribute zero nutrition. They contribute significantly to the frosh fifteen weight gain.
- Support underage friends. Do not encourage them to drink. Respect their decision to refrain from drinking. Respect the decision of all who wish to refrain from drinking. They do not have to provide an explanation. It is rude and an invasion of privacy to press for one.
- Do not walk home alone in the dark. Make use of the campus walk-home service.
  » Think about it. This service is available because various incidents have happened on campuses many times before. If you have been drinking, your ability to scream and defend yourself may be lowered. Refer to Chapter 3.1.
- At a party, pour your own drinks to manage the amount you are drinking.

---

47 First National Study of Drug Use Among University Students Released by the Centre for Addiction and Mental Health. Based on data gathered from 7800 undergraduate students in 16 universities across Canada.
48 Ibid.

Do not leave your drink unattended and avoid being subjected to "jokes" from "friends." Some misguided individuals think it is funny to add extra alcohol or other drug substances to your drink to see how you react. These are the types of "friends" from which you need to distance yourself.

» There are even more serious reasons to protect your drinks when out in public. There have been occasions when drugs have been added to the drinks of female party participants with the intent of lowering their inhibitions and facilitating rape[49]:

» The most frequently used date rape drug is Rohypnol, the brand name for flunitrazepam. It is commonly known as "Roofies," "ruffies," "roche," "R-2," "rib" and "rope";

» Rohypnol is similar to Valium but much more potent. The drug produces a sedative effect, as well as amnesia and muscle relaxation. Sedation occurs 20 to 30 minutes after ingestion and lasts for several hours;

» If roofies are combined with alcohol, marijuana or cocaine, they produce a rapid and very dramatic effect. Some unfortunate young women have reported waking up with no clothes on, finding themselves in unfamiliar surroundings with unfamiliar people, or having suffered a sexual assault;

» In addition to the obvious dangers of unprotected sex, such as pregnancy or a sexually transmitted infection, Rohypnol may lead to respiratory depression, aspiration, and even death, particularly if it is mixed with alcohol or other drugs;

» Roofies can also produce an amnesia-like effect so you may not be able to remember the circumstances under which you took the drug. As a result, investigation of sexual or other assaults where there is the involvement of Roofies may prevent users from remembering how or why they took the drug or even that others gave it to them. This makes investigation of sexually related or other offences very difficult;

» You need to be aware that this could happen to you or a friend;

» It is not happening at every party, but you can't predict who will show up and when it might happen;

» Team up with a friend before every party and ask them to be your second set of eyes. Whether or not you have been drugged, a friend can help you if you have had too much to drink and realize you are losing control;

---

49 Some of the information included in the following four bullet points is based on Staten, C., 1996, 'Roofies', The New "Date Rape" Drug of Choice, downloaded from www.emergency.com/roofies.htm, February, 2005.

» If you start to feel light-headed, tell your friend immediately.

Remember, pour your own drink and never leave it unattended.

- Seek advice from Health Services if you feel you can only relax and have fun by using alcohol or if you are unable to control your usage of alcohol.

Addiction is the continuing, compulsive use of a substance that occurs despite negative consequences to the user. Addiction is a disease—it is chronic, progressive and potentially fatal. Addiction requires professional treatment.[50]

13.5 Street drugs

Many people think marijuana is perfectly safe, but numerous studies show evidence to the contrary. Inform yourself about the 400 chemicals in marijuana and the negative physical and psychological health effects that drug use could have on your body. There are also safety and legal consequences. Review the following Web sites:
http://www.drugwise-droguesoisfute.hc-sc.gc.ca/index_e.asp
www.raisingourkids.com/cms/index.php?page=articles&id=613
www.canadian-health-network.ca.

Forty-seven percent of students reported using cannabis at some point in their lives and 28.7 percent used cannabis during the previous 12 months.[51]

- Each individual is affected differently. For some, just a few tokes can zap energy, commitment and focus, which will reduce your ability to stay on track at school.

Perseverance, motivation, self-confidence, acuity of analysis, discernment of complexity and depth of interaction are all diminished when you are stoned. [52]

Calvin White

---

50 A Parent's Guide For the Prevention of Alcohol, Tobacco, and Other Drug Use. Ashbury College. Community of Concern.

51 First National Study of Drug Use Among University Students Released by the Centre for Addiction and Mental Health. Based on data gathered from 7800 undergraduate students in 16 universities across Canada.

52 White, C., Are we helping our kids got to pot?, *The Globe and Mail*, December 4, 2004, page F7.

- Be wary of "hash brownies." You have no idea of the quality, quantity or actual substance that is in them.
- Do not drive if you have used marijuana. Your reactions and abilities are impaired and it is illegal.
- There are many other drug substances in the student environment. The RCMP has an excellent factual site on the use and dangers of chemical drugs: www.rcmp-grc.gc.ca/bc/crops/drug_awareness/index_e.htm

- Seek advice from Health Services if you feel you can only relax and have fun by using drugs or if you are unable to control your usage of drugs.

13.6   Smoking

We all know the mantra: Stop smoking! Do yourself and your loved ones a favour, and consider making the effort to stop. This is the first step towards quitting. Consider the following:

- Smoking is bad for your health;
- Smoking inhibits sports performance;
- Smoking is expensive;
- Smoking makes your clothes, breath and hair smell unpleasant and unattractive to non-smokers around you;
- Second-hand smoke hurts others around you.

Visit the following Web sites for more facts and details on the noxious substances added to cigarettes:

www.stupid.ca

www.gosmokefree.ca

---

53   First National Study of Drug Use Among University Students Released by the Centre for Addiction and Mental Health. Based on data gathered from 7800 undergraduate students in 16 universities across Canada.

54   Ibid.

- Strongly resist the temptation to try a cigarette if you don't already smoke. Once you start it is very hard to quit.
- Seek professional help from your doctor to quit. The longer you wait the harder it will be to stop.
  - » Remove yourself from smoking environments to lessen the temptation. Most smokers say it is hardest to resist when they are in social environments, especially those involving drinking. Team up with another friend who is committed to stop and support each other;
  - » Persevere even if you fall off the wagon;
  - » Refer to Health Canada's Web site which is designed to help you achieve success in your quest to stop smoking: www.hc-sc.gc.ca/hecs-sesc/tobacco/quitting
  - » Or call the smokers help line at 1-877-513-5333.

13.7   Exercise and relaxation

Make some form of exercise a priority in your life. Be proactive and don't wait until you are stressed to consider natural stress relievers.

- Make the gym your first stop of the day. In addition to the benefits of exercise, this approach has the added attraction of showering at the gym, which is often a better choice than competing with roommates for limited shower time and hot water!
- Make a commitment to yourself to engage in one specific activity at the athletic centre on a regular basis.
- Three 30-minute-long aerobic sessions per week are recommended to maintain a healthy heart and body. Some experts say that three ten-minute periods of daily activity are just as healthy.
- There are many direct benefits of exercise:

- » Reduces stress;
- » Increases your energy;
- » Enhances your emotional health;
- » Keeps your heart and body healthy;
- » Regulates your appetite;
- » Has been shown to reduce the risk of certain types of cancer;
- » Is a great way to meet people.

- If you don't wish to participate in sports or work out at the gym, try walking.
  - » A walk in the fresh air after a few hours of studying will clear your head, re-energize you, and improve your focus;
  - » Twenty minutes of walking is better than twenty minutes of staring into space;
  - » Get into the habit of walking to the nearest grocery store in your quest for fresh fruits and vegetables;
  - » Take the stairs rather than the elevator.
- Stand up and stretch your body regularly when you are sitting for a prolonged period of time.

13.8 Solving problems

Be prepared to make an effort at solving problems yourself, but recognize when you need help, and ask for it.

- Before getting too worried about a problem, think about the goals and values you considered in Chapter 1.2. Then reassess the problem.
  - » What is most important to you?
  - » What information are you lacking to guide you?
  - » What are the possible sources of information?
  - » Go and get the information you need to make a decision;
  - » Think about your main alternatives, and the pros and cons of each;
  - » Which of the pros do you weight heavily in the sense that you would really like to achieve them, and

which of the cons do you weight heavily in the sense that you would really like to avoid them?

» Having reflected on the problem, jot down your thoughts, even if only on a napkin in the cafeteria. With your notes in front of you, you have a pretty good chance of making a decision that is good for you. Also, you are much more likely to be able to converse intelligently about your problem with people around you who can help;

» If you have not had to solve a lot of your own problems, even small problems can seem insurmountable, or beyond your capabilities. The truth is that you are very likely quite capable;

» If you are feeling overwhelmed, seek help from Student Services.

13.9 Emotional health

There are highs and lows associated with university life as you push the envelope of your social, academic and athletic skills. Don't be surprised when you experience them. Although the "lows" are never fun, they are part of life, and they are part of what you are learning to cope with on your own at university.

• If you are having relationship or other troubles, discuss them with friends. Talking about your worries alleviates some of the stress and keeps things in perspective.

• A regular exercise program also does wonders for your mind.

• Do not hesitate to seek professional help from your doctor or Health Services if you feel overwhelmed.

» We all feel blue on occasion. However, prolonged feelings of despair can be a sign of depression and you should discuss this with your doctor. A useful Web site to help you recognize signs of depression in yourself or in others is www.mypeaceofmind.ca

» Be aware of warning signs in your friends, and suggest they speak with their doctor;

» Refer to Chapter 16.2 for other sources of help.

13.10 Maintaining your relationships with friends and family

Keep in touch with your friends and family to let them know how you are doing. They will appreciate a brief e-mail or short phone call.

• Let your parents know when you miss them.

» Touch base at times other than when you need help or money;

» If you have moved away from home for the first time, your parents will also be adapting to their new life without you and may find it quite difficult, despite any jokes to the contrary. Make sure they know about student care packages! www.canadian studentcare packages.ca

» If they are worried or hounding you, remember it is only because they care. If you share your experiences with them and let them know you are managing, they will eventually step back and leave you to manage your own life.

13.11 Spirituality

If spirituality is a part of your life, make room for it and nurture it.

- Nurturing your spiritual life can be a great help in keeping you focused on your goals and lending balance to your life.
- If people around you are supportive, then great. If not, think about reducing their role in your life.
- Prayer, meditation or a simple walk alone, appreciating and admiring nature around you, can help reduce stress and keep your life in perspective.
- Most universities have a chaplain on campus to whom you can go for guidance.
- Universities have information about churches, synagogues, mosques or meditation groups that are nearby and many of those have special programs for students.
- There are many forms of non-traditional spirituality. Some people believe that God is a state of each individual's higher consciousness. Others define God as the total realization of personal, human potential. Explore and appreciate other philosophies and viewpoints.

13.12 Committed relationships

In a healthy, committed relationship, your partner is a close friend, someone to confide in, to share experiences with, to support, and to turn to for support. It is for these reasons that a healthy, committed relationship can be very rewarding.

- On the other hand, many relationships can be very draining, both of your time and your emotional health. Many productive days and nights can be wiped out because you are worried about your partner's problems or because you have had a fight.
  - » If your relationship is absorbing too much of your time, consider deferring it until the term is over;
  - » Many students take the attitude that they do not want a committed relationship while they are studying. Honesty with your partner about your level of commitment is critical.
- Even if you are in a close, committed relationship, you should befriend other students. Your friendships with others should not be constrained by a jealous partner.
- If you are not in a committed relationship, you might think a partner would bring you happiness. The truth is, someone else can't bring you happiness. It is up to you. Seeing yourself in a positive light, nurturing your self-respect, surrounding yourself with people who respect and support you, living your own values, and striving to achieve your own goals and ambitions are some of the significant contributors to your happiness. And you have control over them. If you take care of yourself and your happiness, a positive healthy relationship will likely follow.

Fifty-six percent of undergraduate students are in a personal relationship of some kind with about 25 percent of students being in a long-term relationship. Over 40 percent of students report being single and not seeing someone.[55]

---

55   Survey of Undergraduate University Students: University of Winnipeg, 2002, downloaded from http://www.uwinnipeg.ca/index/cms-filesystem-action?file=pdfs/future/cusc.pdf on April 6, 2005.

For First Years, the weeks leading up to Thanksgiving are a time of self-discovery and change. For many, this is the first time that a committed relationship has been put to the test of separation by a long distance. Inevitably, some committed relationships dissolve, and Thanksgiving, when separated couples are reunited after those initial few weeks, is the weekend they may have to face this reality.

13.13 Sexuality

If you are sexually active, have been, or are planning to be, make an appointment with your doctor or Health Services to ensure you are doing everything correctly to avoid pregnancy and sexually transmitted infections (STIs).

- Use condoms to avoid the transmission of STIs. Condoms are not just a "guy thing." Both parties to a sexual relationship are responsible for taking appropriate steps to avoid transmitting or contracting STIs.

Nearly 44 percent of sexually active 20 to 24 year-olds reported sex without a condom, compared with 33 percent of those aged 18 to 19, and 22 percent of those aged 15 to 17.

- You must fully inform yourself on STIs. Take the time to read through Appendix 4. If you want even more detail, browse the following Web sites:
  www.phac-ascomputer.gc.ca/publicat/epiu-aepi/std-mts/condom_e.html
  www.getthetest.ca
  www.thebody.com/cdc/factcond.html
  www.sexualityandu.ca
- Avoid pregnancy by using a supplementary method of birth control in addition to condoms.

Thirty percent of Canadian female college students are estimated to have Human Papilloma Virus (HPV). See Appendix 4 for more details.

- Sex is both physical and emotional. The level of emotional commitment varies widely amongst people. Prior to commencing a sexual relationship:
  » Consider and discuss with your partner the expectations you each have

---

56 Early sexual intercourse, condom use and sexually transmitted diseases; The Daily, May 3, 2005, Statistics Canada.

with respect to your relationship. If you differ significantly, you should make decisions to preserve your emotional well-being and that of your partner. For example, if one partner is casual and the other isn't, you must reconcile this. If you can't, you may have to terminate the sexual relationship;

» Be sensible in the selection of your sexual partners. If you pick a partner who is reputed to have had many one-night stands and you are looking for a committed relationship, it is probably all the more important to discuss your expectations;

» People who truly care about you won't use threats of breaking up or other intimidation to convince you to have sex. If you experience this, think carefully about what you are doing in that relationship.

• Be careful when consuming alcohol or using drugs. Both tend to reduce inhibitions and you may make a decision you will regret later on.

• Sexual intimacy can bring distracting worries. You may want to think about how these worries make claims on your time and attention before engaging in sexual activity. Think about whether there will be room in your challenging and busy new university life for these extra pressures:

» Am I pregnant?
» Have I contracted an STI?
» Is my significant other using me?
» Am I any good in bed?
» Is he or she cheating on me?

• Sexual intimacy can also lead to significant time pressures:

» I have to get to the drugstore now;
» I need to go to Health Services for a prescription;
» I need to get a blood test;
» I need counselling.

Have a frank discussion

with your partner about STIs. Some people find this a difficult or embarrassing topic to address. However, given the seriousness of STIs, the decision to have a sexual relationship carries with it the requirement to discuss STIs with your partner. If you are not mature enough for the conversation, you are not mature enough for sex. It is better to overcome your embarrassment and discuss these issues rather than end up with, or propagate, a possible lifetime infection. A caring partner will respect and appreciate your honesty.

• If you have an STI:

» Speak with your doctor about the available treatments;
» Inquire as to whether you should be tested for any other STIs;
» Ask for guidance about how to initiate the discussion you should have with your partner(s);
» Discuss the protection you should use with your partner.

- If your new partner has been sexually active, insist that he or she get tested for STIs before you have sex. If you have been sexually active, offer to do the same.
- Say no if you are not completely sure you wish to have sex.
- If you are questioning your sexual orientation, speak to your doctor or Health Services. There are many groups to assist you with information and support. If individuals within your social circle are not supportive of your sexual orientation, think about reducing their role in your life.

14. Accommodation

If your "home life" is stable and pleasant, it will be a foundation for the rest of your busy life with all of its academic, athletic, social and other opportunities. Whether you live in residence, in a house or apartment, or at home with your parents, you need to think about what you want out of your "home life" and what you can do to make it the comfortable foundation it should be.

In Chapter 2.5 we indicated that there are a number of possible living arrangements at university, with the main alternatives being to live at home, in residence or in your own home or apartment, and to live alone or with roommates. We discuss these in this chapter.

14.1   Residence

If you can afford it and if there is availability, residence is a good option for most first-year students.

- You will be integrated into frosh week with groups of people from your residence and will meet other new people quickly.
- You will meet lots of interesting people in programs other than your own and from other provinces and countries.

- You will make friends with people sharing the same excitement and apprehension about the term ahead.
- You will free up time that would be spent on housecleaning, cooking and grocery shopping.
- You will save time through the ease of access to campus and to the cafeteria.
- You will avoid some "house problems" that can be upsetting and time-consuming, such as a housemate who "neglects" to pay the rent.
- You may benefit from extra services, such as computer and network support with free virus protection software.
- There is usually some flexibility to change rooms, floors or roommates if you are not happy. Your floor senior or residence don can help you work out alternatives.

Strong self-discipline is required to resist the many distractions and temptations around you.
- Even though quiet-time hours are often established, friends will continually be knocking on your door with suggestions of things to do other than studying.
- There will always be students hanging out in one of the rooms down the hall. You will be tempted to join them.
- You will also lose privacy.
- You will get drawn into the problems that other people have.

Students in university residences were most likely to have reported having had five or more and eight or more drinks per occasion at least once (70.4 percent and 44.2 percent, respectively) compared with students in other types of housing.[57]

Most students move out of residence after the first year, citing the following reasons:
- They are ready for a new experience;
- There are a lot of rules, and having adapted to the university environment, they are ready for more independence;
- They want to have friends over for longer periods of time, and to have large groups of friends over for parties;

---

57   First National Study of Drug Use Among University Students Released by the Centre for Addiction and Mental Health. Based on data gathered from 7800 undergraduate students in 16 universities across Canada.

- They crave their own space away from so many people;
- They are tired of the meal plan and want to be more creative with cooking;
- Despite residence rules, noise violations are frequent and at all hours of the night.

Comments from a First Year in Residence:

On the plus side:

You will get to see a lot of posters and get a lot of internal mail in res, so you're always informed about what's going on around campus, and you don't have to search for that information. People will come to you!! It's a lot of fun to watch TV shows like The O.C. in your common room with a group of people. You can generally always find someone else who's awake late at night if you want to make a snack or just take a short study break with him or her. Res maintenance is usually pretty good about dealing with any problems, such as phones not working, or Internet being down. Internet is really fast. The door of your res room is a great place to introduce yourself to people, even if you're not actually in your room. Decorate to your heart's content with funny pictures or comics. Also, hang up a white board so that people can leave you messages as they're going by or so that you can let people know where you are.

On the downside:

You might not be in your first-choice res. For instance, you could get put in a single-sex res. The don on your floor may not be a person you like or look up to, or they may just not be around very often for you to talk to them. There is the possibility that you like your roommate a lot, but you don't get along with the other people on your floor very well. There may be a lot of floor activities that you kind of have to go to, even if you don't want to. Sometimes, res rules state that there are exam quiet hours, like 22 hours of quiet per day for the entire exam period, meaning that you have to stay quiet even when you don't have an exam...and this could be for up to three weeks!! Most likely, you'll have to deal with sleeping in a single bed. Sometimes there aren't ovens in the res, or they're really old and hard to use, which means that you can't make anything fancy, or bake cookies or anything like that.

Zoe, Queen's University, ArtSci '08

14.2   Your home away from home

Residence may be full or you may prefer to rent a room or share a house with some other students.

- Some people prefer to live alone. This is a personal choice that offers more privacy, and complete control over your living and study environment. However, living alone is expensive, and can be lonely, so make sure this really is your preferred living arrangement.
- If you decide to live with friends or other students, choose your housemates wisely, considering the issues detailed in Chapter14.3.
  - » Discuss what will happen if one person wants to move out prior to the expiry of the lease;
  - » Talk about the conditions under which a housemate could be asked to leave;
  - » Discuss how you will handle a twelve-month lease if you intend to vacate during the summer. There may be nobody to sublet to;
  - » Clarify how the rent and utilities are to be paid;
  - » Ask housemates where their money will come from to pay their share of expenses. How reliable is that source of income?
  - » Share expenses such as telephone, cable, and Internet;
  - » Suggest each person use calling cards for long distance calls;
  - » Avoid having utility bills in your name to avoid a bad credit rating if a roommate does not pay their share. Arrange for the housemates to contribute to a fund that can be applied to the last month's bill, or any other unpaid bills;
  - » If any bills are in your name, ensure you remove your name as soon as you move;
  - » Agree on house rules up front as suggested in the House Rules Checklist in Appendix 3, and identify those issues that might be a problem. This checklist can be downloaded from www.universitymatters.ca

14.3   Getting along with roommates

Whether you live in co-op housing,[58] live in residence, share a house, or share a room there are many potential sources for frustration.

- The easiest way to minimize additional stress in your life is to communicate and agree upon house rules up front.

---

58   For more on co-ops, check www.chfc.ca and click on co-ops for students.

- Whether you selected your roommates yourself, or someone else determined them, you should discuss the individual preferences of each roommate, respect each other's wishes, and where possible, make arrangements to accommodate your differences.
- Make a pact to discuss how things are going once a week for the first few weeks. Establish a regular time and location, such as Friday afternoon at the campus coffee shop. This avoids having problems build up to an explosive level before they can be addressed. After a while a monthly meeting should suffice, though it is better to discuss issues as soon as possible after they arise.
  - » Work out compromises right away;
  - » Respect your roommate's wishes if you are requesting accommodations that are outside of the basic agreement;
  - » Accept that your roommate has the right to change his or her mind on an issue that had previously been agreed upon;
  - » Ask a third party to act as an intermediary for you if you are unable to explain your positions to each other;
  - » Accept the situation unless it is intolerable, in which case, speak to your floor don or other friends for advice.
- Residence administrators attempt to pair people with similar interests, but paper descriptions do not always reflect reality. Even if you do the selecting, as would be the case if you were to rent a house, difficulties can arise. Until you live with someone, you will not realize what he or she is really like. A roommate may not even be aware of his or her annoying habits. Sometimes roommates will go through an entire year barely speaking. Others have fun and enjoy each other's company throughout university and become lifelong

friends. Communication is essential and will help you achieve the latter rather than the former.

- If you and your roommate tend to look at the world in very different ways, think about your likely Myers-Briggs personality type and that of your roommate to understand why. Refer to Chapter 12.1.
- Mount a large notice board on the wall in a well-trafficked area of your house, such as the kitchen or near the telephone.
  » Use this as a primary means of communication with each other;
  » Allocate a portion of the board to each person. Put their telephone and other messages there.
  » Carve up the rest of the board into functional areas such as:
    » Missing items;
    » The chore roster;
    » The house rules;
    » Finances.

Try to make meal preparation, or doing the dishes, an opportunity for housemates to meet and talk about what is going on in their lives—an opportunity for social interaction. It is much more fun to put a meal together over conversation with friends than it is to do it alone.

14.4   The challenges of living at home

You might choose to live at home for the first few years of university for financial reasons, for simple convenience, or because you are not ready to handle the challenges of living on your own, together with the challenges of your new academic program. Also, you might prefer, or realize you need, the forced structure of living in your parents' home.

- On the plus side, you will probably benefit from home cooking, a comfortable bed, laundry facilities, the use of a car, computer facilities and the many other comforts of home.
- On the downside, you might feel frustrated if you want more freedom than your parents feel is reasonable. Your peers might be out until the small hours of the morning, but your parents might not appreciate your arrival home at four in the morning. You may also be subjected to an ongoing stream of "advice" concerning your sleeping habits, your studying regime, and your friends. If your parents are financially contributing to your education, they may feel they have a right to ensure you spend your time well.

- While staying in your parents' home you must abide by their rules.

  » Appreciate that it is a privilege to be supported as you continue your studies;

  » Do not treat your home like a hotel. If you live at home, you still have family obligations within the home. Clarify your parents' expectations in this regard.

- Some things to think about and discuss:

  » Do you need to contribute financially for room and board? Completing your budget as detailed in Chapter 15 will help you reach a reasonable compromise;

Have structured family meetings to discuss your parents' expectations and present yours. Reach compromises and ask for the opportunity to show them how you can live independently within their home.

  » Do you need or want "reminders" from your parents to do your academic work?

  » At the very least you should clean up after yourself. Make sure you and your parents understand and agree upon the chores that are your responsibility;

  » How much time can you spend watching TV or playing video games?

  » Make daily arrangements about when you will be home for dinner. If your plans change, call home early. If you come home earlier or later than expected, prepare your own dinner;

  » Is anything in the fridge and pantry off limits?

  » Are you and your friends allowed to drink alcoholic beverages in the house?

  » Discuss the terms for using the laundry facilities at home. When are they available to you? Dragging your clothes to the laundry room at 11p.m. may not be appreciated. Can you use the family's laundry soap? Can you leave your laundry half done on the floor? What about leaving clothes in the dryer?

  » If you have the use of a family car, determine when it is available and what you are expected to contribute for gas and insurance;

  » How many friends can come to your home and on what nights?

  » What are the rules for friends staying over? What are the rules for partners sleeping in your room?

  » Are there any curfews? Are you disturbing light sleepers, younger children or exciting a dog by coming home late?

- » There are probably a number of issues specific to your particular situation that you should add.
- Spend some time with your parents, even if it is just going for a walk once a week.
- If you can afford to, get your own telephone line and answering machine.
- Although you may feel your peers have a "better deal," try to focus on the fact that your living arrangement is helping to get you the education you want. There will always be people with "seemingly more and an easier life," but there are very many more with much less.

If you do live at home, you should make the effort to be on campus as much as possible to engage in your new environment and be as involved in university life as students living in residence or close to campus.

15. Managing Your Finances

People with financial problems often look back on things and ask, "How did I get into this mess?" The answer is, bit by bit. It is amazing how quickly a series of small financial indiscretions accumulates into a big problem.

"How am I supposed to stay out of a financial mess?" The answer to the question is the same, bit by bit. Every time you make a sensible and prudent financial decision, you are putting a brick in the wall of financial solidity. Big strong walls are built one brick at a time.

This is not about getting rich. It is about financial happiness, which at university means living within your means for about eight months until you can get back out there and regenerate your resources. The financial reality of university is probably best expressed by a single statistic: average graduating student debt is $20,000. With

Seventy percent of students have concerns about having sufficient funds to complete their education.[59]

poor financial management, you can easily exceed this amount. The goal is to manage well because it is cumbersome to be saddled with debt when you graduate, which can get in the way of new goals, such as saving for a house and buying a car.

While you are attending university, financial problems are irritating, stressful and time-consuming. You don't want any of these things when you have many more

---

59 Survey of Undergraduate University Students: University of Winnipeg, 2002, downloaded from http://www.uwinnipeg.ca/index/cms-filesystem-action?file=pdfs/future/cusc.pdf on April 6, 2005.

interesting opportunities than you can possibly seize, and way too little time. A little bit of budgeting and planning up front will establish a roadmap that will keep you on the financial straight and narrow, but perhaps more importantly, it will also help keep you happy.

If you think education is expensive, try ignorance.

Mark Twain

15.1   Budget template

Download the budget template that is available on our Web site:
www.universitymatters.ca

15.2   Determining all potential sources of income

- Savings
- Registered education savings plan (RESP) proceeds
- Summer employment income
- Part-time job
- Parental assistance
- Scholarships
- Bursaries
- Loans
- Inheritance
- Investment income
- Income tax refunds
- GST rebates

15.3   Determining all anticipated expenses

Academic expenses:
- Tuition
- Activity fees
- Computer, printer, paper, ink, software
- Textbooks
- Pens, paper, binders and other required supplies

Living expenses:
- Residence
- Meal plan
- Rent
- Utilities (heat, electricity, water)
- Food
- Cleaning materials
- Household items (light bulbs, batteries)
- Phone
- Internet
- Cable TV
- Insurance

Personal expenses:
- Entertainment
  - » Be realistic; you will and you should go out and have fun and this will cost money. It is better to recognize this up front than to pretend it won't happen and be constantly short of cash;
  - » Take cash when you go out and only take what you want to spend.
- Shoes and boots
- Clothes and winter wear
  - » Check out the second hand shops, there are great buys to be had.
- Sports clothes and equipment
- Transportation home

Trips home during the first year tend to be more frequent than in subsequent years. Budget accordingly.

- Local transportation, bus pass
- Car expenses for the lucky few (loan payments, insurance, gas, maintenance, parking)
- Coffee, snacks
  - » Think about these. They add up.
- Haircuts
- Medication (portion not covered by insurance)
- Eyeglasses (may be partially covered by a parent's insurance plan)
- Dental (portion not covered by insurance)
- Cell phone

- Personal hygiene products
- Laundry facilities and detergents
- CDs
- Newspapers and magazine subscriptions
- Gifts
- Vacation
- Child care
- Pet expenses

15.4 Developing plans to address shortfalls

If your budgeting exercise indicates you will run short of cash, you can reduce your expenses, increase your income, or do a combination of both.

- First, you should carefully review your expenses and see where you can cut back.
  » Go through your budget and cut back on discretionary items, such as coffee, snacks, beer and junk food. Rather than buying your lunch at the cafeteria, make it at home;
  » Make do with the clothes you have. Everyone feels great in new clothes but not good enough to beat that sinking feeling when you have to borrow more money. Get into the "poor student" mindset;

I think that something new students need to be aware of is the "real world" after university, where you have to have a car, a place to live, and start paying off student loans! Even from the very beginning, students have to know that university lasts for only four years, and ends pretty quickly!

Jenn, Carleton University,

Arts '05 Honours Political Science and Classics/Religion

  » Cut back other expenses wherever possible. Question whether you really need certain things such as your cell phone. Ask yourself if you can make do without or whether you prefer to accumulate debt;
  » Cut back on gifts. Recipients are happy that you are being thoughtful, and the actual monetary value of the gift is not important. Consider making a coupon book where you offer your services when required. You can have fun with this: "Call me if your date is boring and I'll take over." At Christmas do the same for family members: "I'll do the dishes if you get

on one knee and say please." Check out "Buy Nothing Christmas." It is a national initiative started by Canadian Mennonites and appeals to everyone who wants to reduce the consumerism overload at Christmas: www.buynothingchristmas.org

» Be careful if you consider paring back your food budget. You have to eat nutritiously to maintain your well-being.

• If you have reduced all of your expenses as much as you can, and you still have a shortfall, you will have to find more money.

» Speak to a bank about their student loan programs. Refer to Chapter 2.2;

» Look into a part-time job that will not interfere with your ability to study. Refer to Chapter 3.9;

» Seek help from your parents. This is easier to do if you have a detailed budget showing that you are being judicious with your expenditures. They may be more receptive if you are able to transfer some of your tuition and education non-refundable tax credits to them as a method of repayment. Refer to Chapter 15.6;

» In some universities, short-term emergency loans are available in the last month or two of term to help students who have run out of money. Speak with an advisor in the Financial Aid office of your university. They will be up-to-date with the various options available to you.

32% Thirty-two percent of students report using services for students in need of financial aid.[60]

34% Thirty-four percent of students have debt from student loans; average amount owed is over $12,000.

18% Eighteen percent of students have debt resulting from loans from family or parents; average amount owed is over $7,000.

13% Thirteen percent of students have debt from loans from financial institutions; average amount owed is under $8,000.

7% Seven percent of students have debt from other sources; average amount owed is over $4,000.[61]

60   Survey of Undergraduate University Students: University of Winnipeg, 2002, downloaded from http://www.uwinnipeg.ca/index/cms-filesystem-action?file=pdfs/future/cusc.pdf on April 6, 2005.
61   Survey of Undergraduate University Students: University of Winnipeg, 2002, downloaded from http://www.uwinnipeg.ca/index/cms-filesystem-action?file=pdfs/future/cusc.pdf on April 6, 2005.

- Some students decide to take a year off to build up financial resources. Think carefully about this and speak to the academic advisors and your parents before making this decision.

> **Three percent**
> of students report interrupting their studies for financial reasons.[62]

  - » On the plus side, this relieves financial pressure;
  - » On the negative side, you may delay returning to school for longer than you had expected as you enjoy the benefits of having cash in your pocket. Then you may be tempted to veer off your educational and career plan;
  - » Also when you do return to university you will be joining a group of students who are younger than you.

15.5 Keeping a record of actual expenditures

Most people are surprised at how quickly and easily money disappears…bit by bit.

- Use your *University Matters Student Planner* to write down where you spend your money each week.
  - » For example, if you withdraw $60 from the ATM, note if $20 went to a new CD, $10 to pizza, $10 to cab fare and the balance, which seems to be a loonie and loose change, to miscellaneous;
  - » You don't want to drive yourself crazy tracking every penny. An approximation is fine with "miscellaneous" accounting for the difference. If the "miscellaneous" number becomes too big, pay better attention to what you are spending your change on.

- Know where your money is going.
- Ask yourself if you are happy with how you have spent your cash.
- Make smart spending decisions going forward.

- At the end of each month, use our Budgeting Spreadsheet to record where you spent all your money. This will help

---

62 Survey of Undergraduate University Students: University of Winnipeg, 2002, downloaded from http://www.uwinnipeg.ca/index/cms-filesystem-action?file=pdfs/future/cusc.pdf on April 6, 2005.

you adjust your spending and enhance your budgeting skills going forward. It is downloadable from www.universitymatters.ca

15.6   Tax considerations

Most students will receive a tax refund if they paid income tax, thanks to special deductions and non-refundable credits available to students. So file early! If you net file, you will likely receive the cash in your account within ten days.

Even if your employer did not withhold any tax, you may be eligible for provincial property and sales tax credits, as well as a possible refund of CPP and EI payments. This money is waiting to be claimed, so file your return!

- Another reason for filing an income tax return is that you will start accumulating room for later RRSP contributions. This may not seem important to you now, but as your tax bracket increases you might appreciate the ability to contribute more to your RRSP.
- Ensure you apply for the GST/HST rebate on your tax return if you are 19 or turning 19 that year. You have to be a resident of Canada and 19 or older to receive the GST/HST credit. The payments are made quarterly.
- Consider buying one of the software packages for completing your tax return to ensure you maximize the deductions and credits available to you. You can share the cost of about $40 with a number of friends since some programs do not limit the number of tax filings you can make with a single software purchase if income is below $25,000. Once you are familiar with the program, you can complete a return in five minutes. You could have a great part-time job completing returns for students around you that are eager to get their refund! Try www.quicktax.ca
- The main details applicable to students are summarized below. Go to the CRA Web site for full details on all of these deductions and credits: http://www.cra-arc.gc.ca/tax/individuals/segments/students/menu-e.html
- The most common sources of student income are:
  » Employment income;

- » Tips (If you work in a bar or restaurant and don't declare your tips, you will likely get audited);
- » Investment income;
- » Scholarships, fellowships, bursaries and grants. The first $3,000 of income from these sources is tax-free if you are eligible for the education amount (see below under non-refundable tax credits). If not, only $500 is tax-free;
- » Research grants;
- » RESP proceeds.
- You do not have to claim as income:
  - » GST/HST credits;
  - » Canada Child Tax Benefit payments;
  - » Lottery winnings;
  - » An inheritance.
- Special deductions:
  - » You can claim moving expenses if you move and take a job:
    - » This applies when you first move from home to university, when you move from your home at university to your residence for the summer, and when you return to university again;
    - » The caveats are that the new home must be at least 40 kilometres closer to your job than your old home;
    - » You can only deduct these expenses from the employment or self-employment income you earn at the new location. Insofar as the cost of moving to university is concerned, you can only deduct the expenses to move to university if you earn income at that location.
- If you pay someone to look after your child so you can go to school, you can deduct some of those costs.
- Non-refundable tax credits reduce the amount of income tax you owe. However, if the total of these credits is more than the amount you owe, you will not get a refund for the difference:
  - » Interest paid on student loans can be claimed for loans made to you for post-secondary education under the Canada Student Loans Act, the Canada Student Financial Assistance Act, or similar provincial or territorial laws;
  - » Tuition fees can be claimed, but not activity fees. The amount that can be claimed will be detailed on Form 2202/2202A provided by the university and usually available on-line;
  - » You can claim an education amount of $400 for each whole or part month that you were enrolled as a full-time student, or $120 for each

whole or part month that you were enrolled as a part-time student. The number of eligible months will also be detailed on Form 2202/2202A.

If you cannot use all of the tuition and education non-refundable tax credits, you can transfer a portion of them to a parent who may then agree to give you the resultant savings received on their taxes. Alternatively, you can carry the credits forward to higher earning years.

15.7   Credit cards

Absolutely avoid credit cards unless:
- You have very strong self-discipline to resist impulse purchases;
- You have access to financial resources to pay off the balance in full each month;
- You can tuck it away and only use it for an unexpected expense, such as your glasses breaking.

You will be inundated with pre-approved credit cards, thanks to miscellaneous mailing lists.
- On the plus side:
  - » You will likely be offered a card that has no annual fee;
  - » You will likely be offered a $500 limit that may be increased as you demonstrate your ability to pay off your balance;
  - » Using a credit card and paying the amount owing in full each month will help you build a good credit rating;
  - » If you use a credit card for purchases and to pay bills you receive, in effect you are getting an interest-free loan from the credit card company from the date of payment until the date the balance owing on the credit card has to be paid;
  - » A credit card is handy to have for emergencies and when travelling.
- On the negative side:
  - » It is too easy to charge "one more item." Charging an item for $60 to

Two thirds of Canadian students carry credit cards.

Ten percent of those carrying credit cards report having three or more cards.

The average balance on their cards is just over $1,000.

Twenty percent do not regularly pay off the monthly balance on their cards.[63]

---

63   Survey of Undergraduate University Students: University of Winnipeg, 2002, downloaded from http://www.uwinnipeg.ca/index/cms-filesystem-action?file=pdfs/future/cusc.pdf on April 6, 2005.

your credit card is tempting. Better to ask yourself, "Am I prepared to pull out three $20 bills and pay for this now?"

» It can be hard to resist the temptation to pay only the "minimum balance due." However, the interest rate charged on credit cards is horrendously high if you do not pay the entire balance in full when due. In today's low interest rate environment, you only receive one percent on your savings account but are still required to pay around 18.5 percent on your credit card balances! Perhaps you want to contribute to the bank's profitability: that's your decision!

If you receive your Visa statement and owe $1,000 but can only pay $950 on the due date, you will still be charged interest on the full $1,000 for that month. That's $15 down the drain! Each additional month you are unable to pay the balance in full will cost you additional interest, plus interest on the interest! The compound interest charges accumulate rapidly.

- If you cannot pay off your credit card balance in full, inquire about a loan. Loan interest rates are typically much lower than credit card interest rates. Then cut your credit card into little pieces! Refer to Chapter 2.2.
- If you are unable to make the minimum payments and cannot work out a repayment plan with the bank you may receive a bad credit rating. This will stay on a central database that can be accessed by all providers of credit. A bad credit rating stays on your record for seven years. It will compromise your ability to obtain credit in the future for such things as a cell phone, a car loan or a mortgage. While you might still be able to get a loan, you will probably be charged a much higher interest rate.
    - » You can check your credit rating with Equifax Canada Inc. at 1-800-465-7166 or Trans Union of Canada at 1-800-663-9980;
    - » Review it carefully and make any corrections if the report contains errors. This is the document banks will review the next time you apply for a loan.
- Cash advances on your credit card accumulate interest from the date they are made rather than from the date the credit card balance is due to be paid. Some banks may charge even higher interest rates and additional fees for cash advances.
- Leave your credit card in a safe place in your room if you are going out at night and know you can't resist the temptation to use it.
- Always check each item on your statement to ensure you made each purchase.

- Avoid having automatic charges made to your credit card so that you retain control over charges to your account and your credit rating.

Never again! I had first-hand experience with direct debits to my credit card in my third year of university. I arranged for cell phone charges to be debited directly to my Visa. Shortly thereafter I cancelled my Visa and terminated the cell phone arrangement. The cell provider failed to cancel the arrangement internally with their billing department. The cell provider charged my Visa monthly and since the card had been cancelled, the charge was rejected. Consequently, the cell phone provider also levied a $25 charge for the bounced charge to Visa. I had moved from co-op housing to share a room with a friend. Of course I did not forward my mail.... For some bizarre reason this went on month after month for two years until I was tracked down by a credit collection agency for a $3,000 outstanding bill! The credit collector was rude and intimidating and it took months of calls to the cell phone provider to clear up the misunderstanding. It was awful! I will never again authorize automatic debits to my credit card.

Erin, University of Toronto, Arts '04

15.8   Financial Tips

- Avoid paying additional service charges at ATMs by using your own financial institution's ATMs. You can end up paying $3 per transaction! Pretty expensive if you are only taking out $40. Refer to Chapter 2.1.
- Keep your PIN confidential, do not write it down and avoid using obvious numbers like birth dates or family names. Financial institutions recommend that you change your PIN every year.
- Avoid retail stores that cash cheques for fees. If the cheque is from a reputable source, a friend will probably be willing to cash it for you if you do not have an account. Better still, open a bank account. Refer to Chapter 2.1.
- Resist borrowing money from friends, even if offered. Your debts will accumulate quickly and then when you earn or receive some money you will feel broke instantly when you repay the loan. Try doing without to the extent you can.
- Avoid lending money to friends.
  - » Even if you are sure they have money coming to them shortly from which

they can repay you, it is very difficult for people who are short of money to part with it. Enforcing collection can ruin a relationship;

» Don't let friends know whether or not you have money. You can't lend what you don't have. Be prepared with a ready answer when asked, for example, "I'm sorry I only have enough to get me through the week."

• Always ask if student discounts are available and carry your Student ID card everywhere.

• Stick to your shopping list and resist impulse purchases.

• Shop at second-hand stores. Oftentimes the clothes are as good as new. You have to browse fairly regularly to find the good items. This can be fun with a couple of friends.

16. So Now You Have to Cope...Again

In Chapter 11 we talked about coping when things go wrong. For example, a serious illness could mess up your academic schedule, you could do poorly on an assignment, a paper or an exam, misjudge your workload, or be rethinking major academic choices. Some things can also go wrong in the lives of your family and friends, and if they do, they can have a significant effect on how you feel and how able you are to cope with the rest of your life.

Sometimes, problems can mount up to a level that is beyond your ability to cope. It is important to understand that this can happen to you, a friend, a roommate or a colleague. It is even more important to understand that there is help for you for precisely these situations. It is there for you to use, and you should. You are worth it!

Thirty percent of students reported some current impaired mental health. Women were significantly more likely to report impaired mental health than men (35.2 percent versus 23.6 percent). The percentage reporting impaired mental health decreased as year of study increased, from 34 percent of first year students to 26.1 percent of fourth year students.[64]

---

64 First National Study of Drug Use Among University Students Released by the Centre for Addiction and Mental Health. Based on data gathered from 7800 undergraduate students in 16 universities across Canada.

16.1   Things can go wrong

At university you will face a potential myriad of challenges from various sources such as:

- Academic work
- Friends
- Family
- Finances
- Health
- Relationships

You might feel stressed if you lose control over a portion of your life or if others criticize you.

- If there is a specific problem you need to deal with, seek help from a trusted friend and the issue will probably become more manageable. Refer back to Chapter 13.8.
  - » Taking just one step towards rectifying the problem will relieve some of the stress;
  - » Ignoring the issue will compound the stress levels and the issue may become magnified in your mind and become overwhelming.
- You may have to deal with a significant life event[65] while at university. A significant life event could include such things as parents getting separated

---

65   The Holmes and Rahe Social Readjustment Rating Scale presents a long list of life events that can induce stress. The scale was first published here: Holmes, T. H., and R. H. Rahe, The Social Readjustment Rating Scale, Journal of Psychosomatic Research, 1967; 11 (2): 213-218.

or divorced, or a parent remarrying. A close friend or family member may experience serious injury or be diagnosed with a serious illness. Most difficult is the death of a close friend or family member. In a close community like a student house, or residence floor, you may be affected if one of your peers is facing a significant life event. If you find yourself facing a significant life event, talk to Student Services for support.

- Do not underestimate the stress you might possibly feel as a student juggling many challenges. Very sadly, students do get overwhelmed with despair and in extreme cases overdose on drugs and attempt or commit suicide. The Christmas holiday season and February are seasonally low times for many people. Pay attention to how you are feeling and seek help if you feel you need it.

- Fifteen percent of Canadians suffer with the winter blues and three percent with Seasonal Affective Disorder (SAD), a clinical illness which is coupled with depression. This is attributed to a lack of sunlight and the tendency to stay indoors during cold winter days.

- Ask yourself the following:

  > **Assess whether** you are dealing with a specific problem that you can address, or whether you are dealing with clinical anxiety or depression.

  » Are you feeling tired all the time?
  » Are you having trouble either falling asleep or staying asleep or are you sleeping too much?
  » Have your eating patterns changed? Are you either eating too much or have you lost your appetite?
  » Are you drinking too much alcohol or turning to drugs to feel better?
  » Are you irritable and short with friends?
  » Are you mad at the world?
  » Are you no longer enjoying activities that you used to find fun?
  » Do you feel lonely?
  » Do you have an upset stomach?
  » Do you get frequent headaches, or suffer with heart palpitations or dizziness?
  » Do you suffer with shortness of breath?
  » Have you lost your motivation?
  » Has your ability to concentrate changed? Are you unable to complete simple tasks? Are you finding it difficult to read?
  » Do you keep procrastinating?
  » Do you think everything is your fault?
  » Are you experiencing suicidal thoughts?

- » Have you fallen behind in personal hygiene?
- » Has your libido declined?
- » Have you avoided leaving your house or room for a period that seems unduly long?
- If you answer yes to any of the questions above, do your best to seek help yourself or tell a friend you need professional help right away. Ask that friend to help you find it. Don't try to resolve persistent feelings of depression by yourself. Alternatively, if you have a friend who is struggling with these issues, encourage him or her to speak to a professional immediately.

16.2 Help is available

Homesickness hits hardest in November. This is the time of year when the novelty of your new-found freedom is wearing off, and residence food or cooking your own meals is losing its appeal. You may have partied too much and fallen behind in your work. Final exams are looming. It is easy to feel overwhelmed.

- Don't bottle up your worries. Verbalizing your concerns really helps. Refer to Chapter 13.8.
- Talk with friends.
- Call your parents or siblings. Don't be hindered by thinking your parents will be disappointed with you. Say upfront that you have a problem and ask for their help. If you feel you cannot approach them, turn to another family member.
- Try to take an optimistic outlook. Ask yourself whether the problem at hand will matter five years from now. The phrases, "This too shall pass" and "Time heals" are true.
- Discuss your concerns openly with your doctor or Health Services, the Counselling Centre, Student Services or an advisor you trust.
- Talk to someone senior in your faith.
- Try some stress relievers, for example:
  - » Exercise
  - » A daily brisk walk
  - » Meditation
  - » Yoga
  - » Massage
  - » Pilates
  - » Tai Chi

- » Swimming
- » Fencing
- » Listen to music, or join a choir
- » Socialize and share thoughts with friends
- Seek professional help.
- If you are concerned with the amount of alcohol you or a friend is drinking, review the questions used by Alcoholics Anonymous on their Web site: www.alcoholics-anonymous.org

- If you prefer anonymity, call a Help Line. 1-800-668-6868 Kids Help Phone accepts calls from university students who are feeling down, or struggling with difficult issues: www.kidshelpphone.ca
- The Canadian Mental Health Association (CMHA) has recently released a new study "Your Education – Your Future, the first comprehensive Canadian guide for college and university students with psychiatric disabilities." The report is based on information gathered from colleges and universities across Canada and features first-hand experiences and advice from students with psychiatric disabilities. For many people, the college or university years rank among the most challenging in their lives.
  - » The report is available on-line on the CMHA Web site: www.cmha.ca
    You can also call them for information and assistance at 1-800-463-6273.

Data from Statistics Canada shows that teenagers and young adults aged 15 to 24 experience the highest incidence of mental disorders of any age group in Canada.

- These Web sites provide contact information and a list of crisis centres in every province and territory: www.suicideinfo.ca www.suicideprevention.ca

NOTES

Final Comments: Your Turn

We wrote this book to help you, and we certainly hope we have. We know the book presents a daunting list of suggestions. Few, if any, of us are able to follow all of them, all of the time. This is not the goal. The goal is to follow the ones you need, when you need them the most, and to do what you can with the others. Our goal is also to present suggestions that you can use to guide you when particular circumstances arise.

If you haven't yet, now is the time to check out our Web site at:

www.universitymatters.ca

We have posted for easy access some downloadable items we hope will help you to:

- Set your priorities (Personal Goals Worksheet)
- Plan for your arrival at university (Planning Ahead Checklist)
- Arrive at university with what you need (What to Take With You Checklist)
- Keep track of your finances (Budgeting Spreadsheet)
- Keep up with your studying (Study Protocol Worksheet)
- Study for tests and exams (Exam/Test Study Worksheet)
- Set up a cosy home (House Rules Checklist)
- Manage your nutrition (Vitamins and Minerals Checklist)
- Keep track of office hours (Professors' Contact Details Worksheet)
- Keep track of what you need (Supply Top-Up Checklist)
- Develop a good resume (Resume Builder Worksheet)

The site presents a list of all the telephone numbers and Web sites we mention in *University Matters*. If you see some Web sites you would like to visit, just log on to www.universitymatters.ca, go to the list of links, and click, rather than typing in the sometimes long and complicated web references in the book. The site is also set up to keep you informed of new and upcoming University Matters products.

Now that we have spent thousands of words "talking" to you, we would like you to talk to us. We are very interested in your life experiences in the months leading up to university, and after the term commences. Help us help the First Years who are following in your footsteps. Please:

- Share your experiences, whether positive, negative, humorous, or not, with us so we, and others, can learn from them;
- Let us know if we have failed to address an issue that is important to you;
- Let us know if we have been incomplete, inaccurate, or misleading with respect to any matter we have raised;
- Let us know if you have had any difficulty locating the sources we have cited, or if you know of better sources.

Tell us what you think: e-mail us at yourturn@universitymatters.ca.

NOTES

NOTES

SECTION FIVE
...
Appendices

Appendix 1

What to Take With You Checklist

Look around your parents' house and take note of what you use on a regular basis. This will be a good indicator of the things you will need when you are on your own. Refer to Chapter 2.6 and download this checklist from our Web site: www.universitymatters.ca.

Kitchen

- Cutlery
- Dishes
- Toaster
- Kettle
- Melitta filter cups for coffee lovers
- Coffee and tea
- Cookie trays
- Cutting boards
- Bowls
- Mugs
- Glasses, including wine glasses and corkscrew
- Garbage bin and bags
- Dish drainer
- Mechanical can opener
- Candles and matches
- Flashlight and batteries
- Tinned food
- Food staples in plastic containers
- Healthy snacks

- A couple of sharp knives
- One good, sturdy, non-stick frying pan
- Pots
- Fire extinguisher
- A cooler bag and ice pack (This is handy for carrying nutritious snacks such as yogurt or cheese if you are heading off to study for a long period of time.)

If you have some money left...

- Microwave oven
- Electric can opener
- Griddle
- Coffee maker
- Grilled sandwich maker
- Television
- Hot Pot (If you're moving into residence this is the greatest invention ever, a cross between a kettle and a hot plate! You can boil water for tea, heat up a can of soup or make pasta!)

Bedroom

- A good pillow and duvet (These and a decent mattress are necessary to sleep well. Take a sheepskin mattress cover if you plan on using the mattress provided.)
- Linen (you'll want an extra set!)
- Strong plastic storage containers or wicker hampers (These can double up as tables and are also useful to carry items back and forth when going home.)
- Use under-the-bed storage units to keep stuff orderly and out of the way.
- Bed raisers, to get your bed high enough up off the floor to enable you to use under-the-bed storage units.
- Photographs of family, friends and pets
- Pictures or posters to brighten up your walls
- A laundry hamper
- Fragrant room sprays or aromatherapy oils (Be considerate to those around you who may have allergies.)

Be warned! Laundry advice from experienced students:
- Don't put wet clothes in your pile of dirty clothes because mould grows fast!
- Make sure you have enough money on your laundry card, or enough change in your pocket, to complete all of your washing and drying cycles.
- Bring some reading to do and stay with your laundry to make sure someone else doesn't take it out and dump it on the side. Sometimes others do that even before the cycle is finished!
- Sort your clothes into piles by colours: dark, light, white.
- Wash new coloured items by hand the first time.
- Check all of your pockets. One forgotten tissue will reduce you to tears!

Other

- Old curtains or sheets for window privacy (Large flags, hockey sweaters and favourite T-shirts are also fun. Use a curtain rod or broom handle to hang them.)
- Supply of condoms and other birth control
- Free-standing lamps or table lamps to brighten up your rooms
- Stereo, radio, Walkman, Discman, iPod and music
- Your favourite board games for low-key evenings
- Playing cards
- Your address book
- Eyeglass repair kit
- Sewing kit and safety pins

For fire safety

- Smoke detector and spare batteries
- Carbon monoxide detector and spare batteries

Optional

- Couch
- Tables
- A mirror to reflect light from the window and brighten your room
- Bulletin board for messages

- White board
- Hammer, nails, duct tape and a mini tool kit containing a screwdriver and pliers
- Spare power cords

A whiteboard outside your door in residence or a shared house is really handy for friends to leave you messages as they are going by.

For studying

- Your *University Matters Student Planner*
- A comfortable chair to support your back
- A desk with a good light for studying at night
- A computer or laptop and a printer together with a power bar and possibly an extension cord (Unless you plan on using on-campus computer labs.)
- Blank CDs
- A CD marking pen to label CDs
- In-basket for bills and paperwork to be filed
- Expandable folders
- Binders for each course and a couple of extras
- Three-hole punch
- Lots of paper and pads for taking notes during class
- White and coloured index cards for summary notes, or for cue cards when giving presentations
- Stapler
- Pens, pencils, erasers, highlighters
- Pads of notepaper for telephone messages, etc.
- Yellow stickies or other page markers
- A strong backpack

Bathroom

- First aid supplies with bandages. The St. John Ambulance Web site offers first aid kits for sale. Although the site lists the contents of the kits, which implies one could replicate them by purchasing the listed items, it is usually the case that purchasing the kit is less expensive than buying the individual items: https://mediant.magma.ca/sja/english_catalog/category_display. cfm?Category_ID=2

- Towels
- Headache relief pills
- Throat lozenges
- Prescription medication
- Soap
- Shampoo and conditioner
- Toilet paper
- Toothbrush, toothpaste, floss
- Creams and makeup
- Deodorant
- Shaving supplies
- Hair gel, etc.

Cleaning Supplies

- Broom
- Vacuum
- Dustpan and brush
- Sponge mop
- Cleaning cloths or rags
- Dishwashing soap
- Tea towels
- White vinegar can be used to clean everything!
  www.frugalliving.about.com/cs/tips/a/vinclean.htm
  http://www.stretcher.com/stories/970811c.cfm
  http://www.harvestfields.ca/Cookbooks/Vin/vinegar.htm
- Steel wool scrubbing pads
- Scrubbing brush
- Bleach
- Laundry powder
- Pail
- Toilet bowl brush and cleaner
- A plunger!
- All-purpose cleaner

Appendix 2

Nutrition: The Good and the Bad

Vitamin A is involved in the formation and maintenance of a strong immune system, healthy skin and hair. It also helps us to see in dim light and is necessary for proper bone growth, tooth development, and reproduction.

- Dark-green vegetables, deep-yellow and orange fruits and vegetables, meats, fish liver oils, eggs and dairy products are good sources of Vitamin A.
- Vitamin A can be lost from foods during preparation, cooking or storage:
  - » Serve fruits and vegetables raw whenever possible;
  - » Keep vegetables and fruits covered and refrigerated during storage;
  - » Try to steam vegetables. Braise, bake or broil meats instead of frying.

The B vitamins are a group of eight individual vitamins, often referred to as the B-complex vitamins. They are essential for the breakdown of carbohydrates into glucose, which provides energy for the body, and for the breakdown of fats and proteins, which aids the normal functioning of the nervous system. B6 in particular helps to maintain a high level of brain function, and B12 is used for red cell formation.

- B12 needs to be supplemented for vegetarians.
- Fortified cereals, wheat germ, whole grains, bananas, peanut butter, milk, eggs, cheese, soybeans, legumes, fish, green vegetables, nuts, pork, liver and chicken are all good sources of Vitamin B-complex.

Vitamin C helps our bodies absorb more iron, protects tissues, joints and ligaments against inflammation and is thought to ward off colds. Another benefit is that it regulates the nervous system and helps us handle stressful situations better.

- Vitamin C is found in fresh fruits (especially kiwi, melon, cantaloupe, oranges, grapefruit, tomatoes and berries), citrus juices, leafy greens (especially broccoli and cabbage), potatoes, and red, yellow and green peppers.

Vitamin D helps with the absorption of calcium and builds strong bones and teeth.
- Fifteen minutes of sunshine a day on our skin provides us with a good supply of vitamin D.
- Given our long Canadian winters, milk has been fortified to compensate for the possible lack of daily exposure to the sun.
- Vitamin D is also found in eggs, fish and fish liver oils.

Vitamin E protects vitamin A and essential fatty acids from oxidation in the body cells and prevents breakdown of body tissues.
- Found in fats and oils, meats, poultry, fish, eggs, legumes, carrots, beets, celery, leafy greens, nuts, sunflower seeds, whole grains, wheat germ, corn and soy. Most ready-to-eat cereals are also fortified with vitamin E.

Vitamin K is used in the body to control blood clotting, and is also involved in bone formation and repair.
- Found in cultured yogourt, green leafy vegetables, cauliflower, cabbage, liver, meat, eggs, cereal and fruits.
- Bacteria in our intestines produce Vitamin K, therefore, deficiencies are rare.

Iron re-oxygenates red blood cells, increasing energy and strengthening the immune system.
- An iron deficiency makes us tired, and decreases our ability to problem solve. It causes anemia, and dark circles under the eyes, and can turn our complexion yellow.
- Many women require supplements in order to replace the iron that is lost through menstruation.
- If you are a vegetarian, you should also discuss the need for supplements with your doctor.
- Red meat is an excellent source of iron. Liver is a great source, but ground beef is probably much preferred by the majority. Veal, apricots, cherries, raisins, prune juice, canned clams, eggs, cereals, beans, lentils, chickpeas, nuts, dried fruit, wheat germ, leafy greens and spinach are other good sources.
- The absorption of iron is enhanced with Vitamin C from cereal and vegetable products.

Calcium is needed every day to keep our bones and teeth strong, to ensure proper functioning of muscles and nerves and to help our blood clot.

- Drink lots of skim milk.
- If you are not a milk lover, eat lots of low-fat cheese, yogourt, tinned salmon mashed with the bones, shrimp, clams, sardines, tofu, broccoli, kale, spinach, almonds, brazil nuts, molasses, grapefruit and fortified orange juice.
- Most people think they are getting enough calcium, but the average person loses 400 mg to 500 mg of calcium per day. Calcium deficiency is usually due to an inadequate intake of calcium. When blood calcium levels drop too low, the vital mineral is "borrowed" from the bones. It is returned to the bones from calcium supplied through the diet. If an individual's diet is low in calcium, there may not be sufficient amounts of calcium available in the blood to be returned to the bones to maintain strong bones and total body health. Aim for at least four servings of calcium-rich foods per day.
- You should discuss a calcium supplement with your doctor if you are lactose intolerant or do not enjoy these foods on a daily basis.

Magnesium is required for the development of bones and teeth. It is also used by the nervous system, assists with muscle contraction and activates the enzymes needed for energy.

- Grains, nuts, legumes, apricots, cherries and dark leafy greens are all good sources of magnesium.

Zinc activates enzymes for important cell functions and is used in the production of insulin.

- Zinc is found in meat, liver, poultry, fish, grains, cereal, bread, eggs, shellfish, green leafy vegetables, beets, carrots, cabbage, gingerroot, garlic, oranges, prunes, legumes, barley and nuts.

Selenium is essential to good health and is incorporated into proteins to make selenoproteins, which are important antioxidant enzymes. These enzymes help prevent cellular damage from free radicals that may contribute to the development of chronic diseases such as cancer and heart disease. Selenoproteins help regulate thyroid function and assist the immune system.

- Brazil nuts, grains, wheat germ, oat bran, fish, shellfish, meat, poultry, garlic, cabbage, broccoli, eggs and beans are all good sources of selenium.

Folate helps produce red blood cells, which carry oxygen to the brain, and prevent mental confusion.

- Strawberries, other fruits, raw vegetables, fortified cereals, chicken, beef and lentils are good sources of folate.

Sodium is required for the regulation of fluid balance, contraction of muscles and conduction of nerve impulses. Reducing sodium in the diet may reduce high blood pressure, which can decrease the likelihood of heart disease, kidney disease and stroke.

- We need about 500 to 1,000 milligrams of sodium per day. A daily sodium intake between 1,100 and 3,300 milligrams, being 1/2 to 1 1/2 teaspoons (2 to 7 mL) of table salt is considered safe. On average we exceed the recommended intake by consuming 2,500 to 5,000 milligrams per day.
- The major sources of sodium in our diets are processed foods, and the salt we add to food during cooking or at meals.
- Reading food and medication labels prior to purchase will help you make low-sodium choices.
- Choose foods labeled "low-sodium," "reduced sodium" or "sodium free."
- Use alternative spices and herbs to season your food. Use pepper instead of salt to season your meal.
- Fresh vegetable and citrus juices are tasty seasonings as well.

Dietary fibre may prevent cancer, diabetes, heart disease and obesity.

- Fibre is an indigestible complex carbohydrate found in plants. There are two categories of fibre:
  - » Insoluble fibre is found in most fruits but especially in prunes and vegetables, dried beans, wheat bran, seeds, popcorn, brown rice, and whole grain products such as breads, cereals and pasta;
  - » Soluble fibre is found in fruits such as apples, oranges, pears, peaches, and grapes and in vegetables, seeds, oat bran, dried beans, oatmeal, barley and rye.
- Choose fresh fruit or vegetables rather than juice, and eat the skin and membranes of cleaned fruits and vegetables where possible.
- Choose bran, cereals and whole grain breads daily. Nibbling on bran buds is an excellent way to increase your daily fibre intake. Adding bran to your morning cereal will result in larger, softer stools by bulking up waste and moving it through the colon more rapidly, preventing constipation and possibly colon cancer.

- Eat more fresh foods and fewer processed ones.
- It is better to get fibre from foods rather than fibre supplements, as foods are more nutritious.
- A large increase in fibre over a short period of time may result in bloating, diarrhea, gas and general discomfort. It is important to add fibre gradually over a period of time to avoid abdominal problems.
- An increase in fibre should be accompanied by an increase in water.
- Fibre makes us feel full; therefore, food intake will be less.

Trans fats are bad fats that raise cholesterol and are linked to heart disease. About 40 percent of products in supermarkets contain them. The Canadian government has recently announced the formation of a task force to develop recommendations and strategies for reducing trans fats in Canadian foods to the lowest levels possible.
- Check labels for the words "partially hydrogenated" or "shortening." Avoid these foods. Partially hydrogenated oils are used in thousands of products, including cakes, cookies, other baked goods and many diet and so-called "health" foods.
- Before ordering in restaurants, check whether they use partially hydrogenated oils when cooking, and avoid such foods.

Saturated fats are the very unhealthy fats. They make the body produce more cho-lesterol, which may raise blood cholesterol levels. Excess saturated fat is related to an increased risk of cardiovascular disease.
- Saturated fats are usually solid or almost solid at room temperature.
- All animal fats, such as those in meat, poultry and dairy products are saturated. Processed and fast foods also contain saturated fats.
- Vegetable oils also can be saturated. Palm, palm kernel and coconut oils are saturated vegetable oils and should be avoided. Check the labels on cracker boxes since many contain saturated oils.

Eating foods high in dietary cholesterol tends to raise the level of blood cholesterol.
- Cholesterol is found in all animal products, such as meat, poultry, seafood, eggs and dairy products. It is especially high in lobster, egg yolks, and organ meats such as liver, brains and kidneys.
- Vegetable products do not contain cholesterol, but they may be loaded with fat. Labels stating "no cholesterol" on food packages can be misleading and should alert you to look at the nutrition information to determine the amount of fat and saturated fat in the contents.

Caffeine is a mild stimulant to the central nervous system, cardiac muscle, and respiratory system. It is a diuretic and delays fatigue.

- Caffeine is found in coffee, tea, cola, chocolate, guarana-based energy drinks and some medications.
- A cup of strongly brewed coffee or tea has more caffeine than a weakly brewed cup.
- Coffee has two to three times more caffeine than tea. For more information on caffeine content, check this Web site: www.wilstar.com/caffeine.htm
- Caffeine increases calcium loss in the urine. Here is what the Osteoporosis Society of Canada has to say about it:

"**Most experts** agree that two to three cups of coffee, tea or cola a day is probably not detrimental if calcium intake is adequate. If you consume more than four cups a day, have at least one glass of milk for every cup of caffeine-containing beverage (or make your coffee a café latté)."[66]

- Here is a basic primer on caffeine[67]:
- » Although it is not addictive, it can be habit-forming. Reducing caffeine may make you irritable, unable to focus, nervous, restless, sleepy, or may result in headaches or nausea;
- » Moderation is the key. Caffeine's effects vary according to each individual, so pay attention to how you feel. When your body has had too much caffeine you may experience frazzled nerves and poor sleep patterns;
- » Cut back gradually by eliminating a drink a day rather than going "cold turkey." You can also mix coffee containing caffeine with decaffeinated coffee, gradually reducing the caffeine ratio over time;
- » Try herbal tea, hot or cold cider, or decaf coffee. Some people enjoy drinking plain hot water.

Coffee does not sober you up after drinking alcohol.

---

66   About Osteoporosis, The Osteoporosis Society of Canada, downloaded from http://www.osteoporosis.ca/english/About%20Osteoporosis/Nutrition/Calcium%20Requirements/default.asp?s=1, March 2005.
67   The material in the following five bullet points is partially based on the article, "Caffeine," McKinley Health Centre, University of Illinois at Urbana-Champaign, downloaded from http://www.mckinley.uiuc.edu/health-info/drug-alc/caffeine.html.

Appendix 3

House Rules Checklist

Sleeping habits:
[ ] When do you go to bed?
[ ] When do you like to get up?
[ ] Do you need a light on at night?
[ ] Do you like music on the radio as you fall asleep or wake up?
[ ] Do you like to leave the window open?
[ ] Do you snore, grind your teeth or talk in your sleep?

Social habits:
[ ] When are visitors welcome?
[ ] What is acceptable for sleepovers by friends or partners? Once or twice might not matter, but it is a different story when the significant other "moves in" and drinks all of your OJ;
[ ] How many visitors at once?
[ ] What time must they leave by?
[ ] Can your bed be used if you are not coming back that night?

Common courtesy:
[ ] Respect the privacy of others by arranging "Do Not Disturb" signals;
[ ] Can you handle a roommate who smells of smoke?
[ ] Agree on what kinds of pets are permitted if your landlord allows them. Respect the allergies of others;
[ ] Agree upon smoking areas if required;
[ ] Agree on TV usage if you are sharing the TV;
[ ] Can you handle a roommate who drinks excessively and gets sick?
[ ] Monitor the hot water supply for showers; if necessary, develop a schedule, which is considerate of each other's needs.

Potentially annoying habits:
- [ ] Do you have any obsessive-compulsive tendencies?
- [ ] Do you crack your fingers?
- [ ] Do you mutter or hum when you are concentrating?

Need for privacy:
- [ ] Do you prefer to change in private?
- [ ] Do you like talking about your studies or your personal life, including your family and relationships?

Study habits:
- [ ] Quiet time specifically for studying should be established and respected;
- [ ] Agree which evenings and at what hours loud music is allowed. Outside of those hours, there should be no exceptions. Or agree your house is a party zone and be prepared to make plans for an alternate space to study;
- [ ] Do you like to study early or late?
- [ ] Can music be on? If so, how loud?
- [ ] If you are sharing a room, determine how late the lights can stay on.

Need for order or chaos:
- [ ] Can you put up with a mess?
- [ ] Does the room have to be clean and orderly?
- [ ] How often should your living space be cleaned?
- [ ] How often should the bathroom be cleaned?

Prepare a chore roster:
- [ ] Identify what is to be cleaned, how often and by whom;
- [ ] Identify the date by when the chore must be done;
- [ ] Rotate responsibilities;
- [ ] Even if it is a specific person's responsibility to clean a room, tidy up after yourself. Clean your dishes, wipe the sink, and wipe the toilet seat. Then the assigned cleaner can do a better cleaning job;
- [ ] You are responsible for tidying up after your guests, even if they have been sick!

Rules to prevent theft:

[ ]   Consider whether you should lock your room or at least your valuables. Consider the signal this sends to others;

[ ]   Do not hang keys inside the front door, especially if they are within reach of a window;

[ ]   Do not leave money lying around.

Decide upon shared meals or separate meals:

[ ]   Develop a cooking roster if shared meals are frequent;

[ ]   Decide which staples can be purchased together and shared;

[ ]   Label shelves in the fridge for individual food purchases and respect rules about "borrowing" food;

[ ]   Designate shelves in the cupboards for individual purchases;

[ ]   Identify and respect any food allergies.

Sharing and borrowing rules:

[ ]   Must you replace what you use?

[ ]   Are some items off limits?

[ ]   Must the other person ask first?

[ ]   What if something is borrowed and damaged?

Appendix 4

Contributed by
Dr. Alison Trant M.D.
Family Practitioner, Ottawa

Sexually Transmitted Infections (STIs): The Truth

An STI is a Sexually Transmitted Infection. These infections were most commonly referred to in the past as STDs or sexually transmitted diseases. The term STI is now used because the word infection includes cases without symptoms, referred to as asymptomatic, as well as those with symptoms.

Many STIs can be present without symptoms. You may not have any symptoms; therefore, you will not know if you have picked up an infection, or when. This also means your partner may have an infection and not know it; therefore, he or she may unknowingly be infecting you.

The total number of people with incurable STIs in the US is over sixty-five million with fifteen million new cases per year of which only a few are cured. Two-thirds of these cases are in people under the age of twenty-five, one quarter of whom are teens.

There is a lack of widespread screening.

Reportable STIs such as Gonorrhea, Syphilis, Hepatitis B, Chlamydia and HIV must be reported to the Canadian Public Health department, so that they can try to trace the contacts and have them treated.

Risk factors:

- Being sexually active;
- Being less than 25 years old, especially if you have had prior multiple sexual partners;
- Having a new partner in the last two months;
- Having more than two partners in one year;
- Not using condoms;
- Having sex with prostitutes;
- Using intravenous (IV) drugs;
- Males having sex with males;
- Using alcohol and drugs, which can affect your ability to make wise decisions and leave you vulnerable. Sometimes it is hard to say no to others. Think about this ahead of time so you can be prepared for these situations.

How to decrease the risk:

- Abstain;
- Have only one partner, who is sexually active only with you;
- Carry condoms at all times if you think you may be sexually active. Follow the manufacturer's directions for discarding them periodically, as they deteriorate if stored in a wallet or pocket for too long;
- Use condoms all the time, together with another method of birth control. Using condoms "most of the time" is not sufficient;
- The practice of "serial monogamy" is not low-risk. Serial monogamy is having one partner at a time, but changing the partner after a period of time e.g., six months, one year, or longer;
- Ask your doctor for screening tests; have your partner do the same;
- Have regular check-ups including pap smears for women;
- Ask your doctor for the Hepatitis B immunization;
- If you do not feel comfortable talking with your family doctor, go the university health centre or the local STI clinic, which are more anonymous;
- Say no, if that is what is right for you!

Bottom line:

- The only way to avoid an STI is to abstain or to be in a truly monogamous relationship between two uninfected partners;
- Many people experience shame, anger, fear and worry about the negative impact disclosing an STI may have on their future relationships;
- It is essential to be honest with your partner and to be proactive discussing

STIs. Some people are too embarrassed to discuss STIs with their partner even if they know they have an infection. A few don't care if they pass the infection on since they are angry that they have it or are just plain selfish;

- Honesty and education of partners, as well as use of support groups, can be helpful. For more information: www.ashastd.org/stdfaqs/index.html

Specific Sexually Transmitted Infections

Human Papilloma Virus (HPV)

- HPV is the most common sexually transmitted infection.[68]
- It is estimated to be present in 30 percent of Canadian female college students. Prevalence is highest in those aged less than 25 years.[69]
- There are 80 types of this virus: 28 affect the genital tract. Most are asymptomatic.
- One person can have more than one type of HPV. This virus has a long and varied incubation period.
- The low-risk types cause raised genital warts.
- Certain types cause a higher risk of cervical cancer in women. This takes years to develop and can be detected early through regular Pap smears.
- Symptoms / Complications:
  » The warts can appear as one or more flat bumps which are flesh-coloured or white. They can be small or very large, adopting a cauliflower-like appearance;
  » The warts may be located on the perineum, which is the outer genital area, including the vulva, as well as on the groin, cervix, scrotum, penis or peri-anal area;
  » People can have one or more episodes. If a wart is present, the infection is considered to be active. The infection is called latent if the virus is present without symptoms. In effect, the virus is sleeping or dormant in the skin cells;
  » Without treatment, the warts may stay the same size, grow or disappear on their own.
- Transmission:
  » It may take weeks, months or years after exposure for a wart to appear;
  » It is possible to have the virus and never have a wart;

---

68 American Social Health Association, Facts and Answers about STDs. Retrieved from http://www.ashastd.org/stdfaqs/index.html, January 10, 2005.
69 Public Health Association of Canada, STD Epi Update, Infectious Syphilis in Canada. Retrieved from www.phac-aspc.gc.ca/publicat/epiu-aepi/std-mts/infsyph_e.html, January 10, 2005.

- » Skin to wart contact is required to contract the virus vaginally, anally, or more rarely, orally. This can happen even if the warts are not visible. Thus, a person can spread the virus without knowing that they have it;
- » These types of HPV don't cause warts elsewhere on the body; warts on other body parts such as feet and hands cannot be spread to the genital area.
- Diagnosis:
  - » Your doctor should assess your symptoms;
  - » Acetic acid can be painted on the surface of the wart or cervix to help the doctor see them. Examination under a special magnifying lens called a colposcope is useful;
  - » There are no blood tests commonly used at this time;
  - » Sometimes effects of the virus are seen on Pap smears in women.
- Treatment:
  - » Removal of the wart using liquid nitrogen, podophyllin, trichloroacetic acid, laser, electrocautery or surgery that requires a physician;
  - » There are some at-home treatments patients can use which require a prescription. Aldara/imiquimod is a topical cream used three times a week for a maximum of four months.
- Prevention:
  - » Condoms help but do not offer full protection because they do not cover all areas. Use them anyway!
  - » Risk is much lower in long-term monogamous relationships.
- Impact on Pregnancy:
  - » Usually genital warts do not pose a big problem during pregnancy and at delivery;
  - » The warts can grow larger during pregnancy, so it is best to have any visible warts treated before pregnancy if possible;
  - » In some instances, newborns exposed to HPV develop tiny growths in the throat. It is so rare for this to occur that vaginal delivery is considered safe.

Herpes Simplex Virus (HSV)

- This is the second most common viral STI. It is a lifelong infection that is relatively harmless, but it can have serious psychological impact.
- The virus lives in the body, often without symptoms or with only occasional symptoms in what is referred to as a period of latency. The virus travels the nerve roots and stays there where it may activate, causing symptoms at a later date.

- It causes recurrent skin blisters and pain. There are two types: HSV 1, which usually occurs on the mouth and can be transmitted to the genital area, and HSV 2, which causes genital lesions.
- Forty percent of lesions cultured are due to HSV 1.[70] HSV 1 generally has a better prognosis since it can be milder and often there are fewer recurrences. Seventy-five percent of people testing positive for antibodies to this virus have no symptoms.[71] In one study done in British Columbia the prevalence of HSV 1 was found to be 58.9 percent; 17.3 percent of people in the study were positive for HSV 2. This number increased to 28 percent by age 44;[72]
- The numbers are even higher in the United States, where prevalence of HSV has increased 30 percent in the last 20 years.[73] Eighty percent of Americans have HSV 1, which is oral herpes; 25 percent have HSV 2,[74] which is genital herpes. One million people per year are infected. There is no cure.
- Symptoms / Complications:
  - » Ninety percent of people infected with this virus are unaware of their infection;
  - » Symptoms can occur within days, weeks, months or years of exposure, so it can be hard to know when and from whom the virus came. If there are symptoms in the first outbreak, they occur within two to 21 days post-contact;
  - » Symptoms include painful blisters, ulcers, or red skin located on the vagina, vulva, anus, penis, scrotum, buttock, thigh or face. Sometimes there are enlarged tender lymph nodes near the infected area, e.g., in the groin. As well, an infected person may have flu-like symptoms. These usually last 10 days;
  - » Recurrences are less severe with fewer of the generalized symptoms such as the flu or enlarged lymph nodes. Infections can be mistaken for abrasions, recurrent "yeast infections," jock itch, ingrown hairs or hemorrhoids;
  - » Transmission is through direct skin-to-skin contact, often through mucosa, the very thin, moist skin of the mouth and genital areas. It can be spread via oral sex or intercourse, even if there are no symptoms present. The virus can be transmitted in both symptomatic and asymptomatic individuals;

---

70 Public Health Association of Canada, Sexual Health and STIs, Condoms. Retrieved from www.phac-aspc.gc.ca/std-mts/condoms_e.html, January 10, 2005.
71 Patrick, Wong & Jordan, 2000.
72 Patrick, Wong & Jordan, 2000.
73 Patrick, Wong & Jordan, 2000.
74 American Social Health Association, Facts and Answers about STDs. Retrieved from http://www.ashastd.org/stdfaqs/index.html, January 10, 2005.

- » It is a fragile virus; you cannot pick it up from inanimate objects like toilet seats;
- » The first outbreak can be severe, but the infection can also be asymptomatic and go unnoticed.

- Diagnosis:
  - » It is best to get a culture diagnosis, which should be done within the first forty-eight hours of the outbreak, to avoid false negatives. The number of outbreaks varies: the average is four to five per year; the first episode is the worst. There are generally more outbreaks in the first year and then the recurrences decrease in number over time. Outbreaks can be triggered by illness, poor diet, stress, friction, surgery and treatment with steroid medication. The best way to reduce outbreak frequency is to avoid stress where possible, get adequate rest, maintain good nutrition and exercise regularly.

- Treatment:
  - » There is no cure. There are good treatments available to decrease symptoms and duration of an outbreak. See your doctor at the beginning of the outbreak and try to obtain repeats of the antiviral medication to have on hand to start at the first sign of a recurrence. Valtrex, Famvir or Zovirax are often prescribed, with the most common side effects being headache and nausea. Usually they are well-tolerated;
  - » You may consider daily suppressive treatment if you have more than five outbreaks per year. These medications have also been shown to decrease transmission rate by 50 percent.

- Prevention:
  - » Decrease your risk of transmission by avoiding oral sex if one partner has blisters;
  - » Use condoms or avoid intercourse if there are any symptoms;
  - » Communication with your partner is essential:
  - » In a mature intimate relationship, one should feel comfortable and conscientious enough to openly share information about sexually transmitted infections. The social and emotional impact of this infection is significant. Educating partners about the natural history of the infection can help. There are also support groups available;
  - » Helpline Ontario 1-800-668-2437 (English);
  - » For other provinces or French numbers see www.phac-ascomputer.gc.ca/std-mts/phone_e.html.

- Impact on Pregnancy:
  - » Rarely, HSV can be transmitted to newborns. Mothers usually pass on antibodies to HSV. The biggest risk of transmission is with having a first episode in the third trimester of pregnancy. If there are visible symptoms at the time of delivery, a C-Section should be performed.
- For more information, visit www.herpeshealth.com or telephone 1-866-252-4666

Chlamydia

- Chlamydia is the most common bacterial sexually transmitted infection in North America.
- Its worldwide incidence is estimated at 19 million.
- It is the most common reported communicable disease in Canada.
- Chlamydia is curable if diagnosed and treated appropriately.
- It affects 15- to 29-year-olds most commonly, females more than males with a 3:1 ratio.
- Two-thirds of the cases in Canada occur in the 15- to 24-year-old age group. After decreasing in prevalence in the 1990s, it has increased by 30 percent to a rate of 146 cases per 100,000 people in Canada in 2000. Newer numbers show a rate of 188.2 cases per 100,000 in 2003.[75]
- People who have been infected will remain infectious until they are treated, and the infection may persist for years. Once a person is treated, they can be reinfected if exposed again.
- It is a good idea for all sexually active women under 25 years of age to ask their doctor for screening.
- Symptoms / Complications:
  - » There are usually no symptoms;
  - » 70 percent of infected females and 50 percent of infected males have no symptoms;[76]
  - » If they develop, symptoms will be present one to three weeks post-exposure. The bacteria can infect the eyes, rectum, vagina, fallopian tubes, urethra, mouth and throat. Infection of the mouth or throat usually has no symptoms. Eye infection will cause discharge and pain. In females, symptoms can be new or different vaginal discharge, pain with urination, pain with intercourse, abnormal menstrual bleeding, bleeding after

---

75 Patrick, Wong & Jordan, 2000.
76 Public Health Association of Canada, Sexual Health and STIs, Condoms. Retrieved from www.phac-aspc.gc.ca/std-mts/condoms_e.html, January 10, 2005.

intercourse, and if the infection spreads into the fallopian tubes, low back pain, abdominal pain, nausea and fever;

» Males are most often asymptomatic but can have penile discharge, itch inside the penis, pain with urination, and pain or swelling of the testicles;

» Men can develop prostatitis, urethral scarring, epididymitis and infertility;

» Pelvic inflammatory disease, an infection of the tubes, can be caused by Chlamydia. This is a common cause of female infertility;

» The infection can also progress to infect the bladder and cervix in females;

» A disorder called Reiter's Syndrome causes arthritis, eye inflammation and urinary tract symptoms. It is caused by Chlamydia.

• Transmission:

» The bacterium Chlamydia Trachomatis, targets mucous membranes and is transmitted through anal or vaginal intercourse, less so by oral intercourse;

» Contact with infected body fluid is all that is required, so that even without full penetration, the infection can be spread;

» Touching your eyes with recently contaminated hands can infect your eyes;

» It cannot be spread by contact with toilet seats or by shaking hands.

• Diagnosis:

» Chlamydia can be tested for in the doctor's office using either a urine test or swabs;

» If the risk exists for Chlamydia, you should also be tested for other STIs.

• Treatment:

» Antibiotics such as Zithromax or doxycycline provide a cure;

» Partners must be identified and treated also;

» This disease must be reported to Public Health. The infected person should abstain from sex until the treatment is complete. Women should have repeated testing done three months after treatment, as there is a high rate of reinfection.

• Prevention:

» Latex condoms for vaginal and anal sex used at the beginning of sexual contact can prevent transmission;

» A condom can be cut and laid flat on the female genitalia for oral sex.

• Impact on Pregnancy:

» Infected mothers can transmit the infection to the eyes or lungs of newborns at birth.

Gonorrhea

- This is the second most common bacterial STI in North America.[77] Unfortunately, it is increasing in prevalence, after having decreased over a twenty-year period; its prevalence has increased by 60 percent since the late 1990s.[78]
- There are over 650,000 new cases reported per year in North America. The rate of infection in 2002 was 23.5 cases per 100,000 people; 26 cases per 100,000 in 2003 and was projected to be 27.9 cases in 2004.[79] The rate of increase has been highest in males over 30 years of age, although the infection is most common in 15- to 24-year-olds.[80] The increase is partly due to the emergence of resistance to antibiotics in some strains of the bacteria.
- Symptoms / Complications:
  - » Most often this infection is asymptomatic;
  - » If symptoms develop, they usually do so within two to seven days of exposure but can present later, up to 30 days post exposure;
  - » Symptoms in men include yellow-white discharge, painful urination, increased frequency of urination and testicular swelling;
  - » Women can have yellow discharge, abnormal vaginal bleeding, painful and frequent urination, painful intercourse, low back pain or abdominal pain, indicating the spread to the uterus or fallopian tubes, nausea and fever. These symptoms are similar to those of Chlamydia;
  - » Ninety percent of individuals with rectal or anal infection have symptoms of fever, itch, discharge and pain with bowel movements;
  - » Throat and mouth infections cause red, sore throats;
  - » Conjunctivitis, an eye infection, produces red, itchy eyes with discharge;
  - » As is the case with Chlamydia, long-term complications can be significant;
  - » There is also a risk of systemic infection, Disseminated Gonorrheal Infection, in which the bacteria gets into the bloodstream and infects other parts of the body, causing fever, arthritis, skin lesions, meningitis and endocarditis (a heart infection).
- Transmission:
  - » The bacterium, Neisseria Gonorrhea, targets the mucosa of the endometrium, the lining of the uterus, the cervix, vagina, urethra,

---

77 Public Health Agency of Canada, Home: Publications: Epi Update 2004, Chapter 2 HIV/AIDS Epi Update – May 2004. Retrieved from http://www.phac-aspc.gc.ca/publicat/epiu-aepi/epi_update_may_04/2_e.html, January 10, 2005.

78 Patrick, Wong & Jordan, 2000.

79 Public Health Agency of Canada, Centre for Infectious Diseases Prevention and Control, Sexual Health and Sexually Transmitted Infections Section. Reported cases and rates of notifiable sexually transmitted infections from January 1 to March 31, 2004. Retrieved from http://www.phac-aspc.gc.ca/std-mts/std-cases-casmts/index.html, January 10, 2005.

80 See preceding footnote.

fallopian tubes, anus, rectum, eyelids and throat;

» It is spread by oral, vaginal or anal intercourse when the mucosa is exposed to infected body fluids such as secretions and semen;

» It can be spread from mouth to penis, penis to mouth, anus to mouth, and vagina to mouth even without full penetration of the penis or tongue. It is not usually spread from mouth to vagina or mouth to anus. Anal gonorrhea can be contracted without anal intercourse due to the spread of bacteria from the vaginal area. Hands contaminated with infected body fluids can infect eyes;

» It cannot be contracted from toilet seats.

- Diagnosis:

» Because of frequent lack of symptoms, people at risk should request testing;

» Throat, vaginal, rectal and urethral swabs can provide the diagnosis;

» This is an infection that must be reported to Public Health so that contacts can be notified and treated.

- Treatment:

» Antibiotics such as Suprax, Cipro or Zithromax can provide a cure;

» Usually an antibiotic that would also treat Chlamydia, if present, is given as well;

» Retesting after treatment is a good idea as there is increasing resistance to some antibiotics;

» Avoid intercourse until after treatment and retesting are complete.

- Prevention:

» Use condoms. If infected, tell your partner(s) and be treated. Go to your Health Services or a local STI clinic for screening if you are at risk or think you might be infected.

- Impact on Pregnancy:

» The infection can be transmitted to a newborn at birth, causing a severe systemic infection;

» In addition to the risks listed for Chlamydia, women infected with Gonorrhea suffer an increased risk of miscarriage in early pregnancy.

Human Immunodeficiency Virus (HIV)

- HIV is a virus that causes an infection that leads to Acquired Immune Deficiency Syndrome (AIDS), which is fatal. This fragile virus cannot survive outside the body; it must enter the bloodstream to infect humans.

- After infecting someone, the HIV virus weakens the immune system over a period of years. When the infected person becomes unable to fight off infections, the syndrome is called AIDS. This usually occurs about 10 years after the initial infection.

- A person can live a number of years with HIV without having symptoms and thus may unknowingly infect others.

- AIDS is a chronically progressive syndrome; individuals easily become infected with opportunistic infections that take advantage of a weakened immune system. These infections can be very serious and often cause death. The infected body is also more susceptible to cancers.

- While treatment for HIV and AIDS has made many advances in recent years, there is no cure.

- Medication can prolong and improve the quality of life of infected people.

- HIV does not occur just in homosexuals.

- Men having sex with men account for 77 percent of adult male AIDS cases, and 70 percent of HIV-positive tests in adult males but only 40 percent of all new HIV infections.[81]

- In 1996, there were 40,000 people living in Canada with HIV. After a decreasing number of new cases of HIV in 1995-1998, the numbers levelled off in 1999-2000.[82] By the end of 2002, it was estimated that 56,000 Canadians were infected with HIV and AIDS; of these, 58 percent of cases were associated with men having sex with men.[83]

- It is estimated that 30 percent of infected individuals are unaware of their infection.[84]

- Intravenous (IV) drug users in Canada account for 16.7 percent of adult HIV and AIDS cases as of July 2003 or 30 percent of new infections.[85]

- Incidence in women due to heterosexual contact or IV drug use is on the increase. In 2002, they represented 25 percent of positive HIV reports.[86]

81 Public Health Agency of Canada, Home : Publications : Epi Update 2004, Chapter 1. HIV/AIDS Epi Update – May 2004. Retrieved from http://www.phac-aspc.gc.ca/publicat/epiu-aepi/epi_update_may_04/1_e.html, January 10, 2005.
83 Patrick, Wong & Jordan, 2000.
83 Public Health Agency of Canada, Home: Publications: Epi Update 2004, Chapter 2 HIV/AIDS Epi Update – May 2004. Retrieved from http://www.phac-aspc.gc.ca/publicat/epiu-aepi/epi_update_may_04/2_e.html, January 10, 2005.
84 See preceding footnote.
85 Public Health Agency of Canada, Home: Publications: Epi Update 2004, Chapter 11 HIV/AIDS Epi Update – May 2004. Retrieved from http://www.phac-aspc.gc.ca/publicat/epiu-aepi/epi_update_may_04/11_e.html, January 10, 2005.
86 Public Health Agency of Canada, Home: Publications: Epi Update 2004, Chapter 5 HIV/AIDS Epi Update – May 2004. Retrieved from http://www.phac-aspc.gc.ca/publicat/epiu-aepi/epi_update_may_04/5_e.html, January 10, 2005.

- Symptoms:
  - » Symptoms do not usually occur until another infection occurs. There may be generalized symptoms such as weight loss and fatigue.
- Transmission:
  - » HIV is spread by direct sexual contact with anyone who has HIV;
  - » Heterosexual transmission is increasing in Canada and is the primary method of transmission in the world;
  - » Infection also occurs through exposure to infected body fluids: blood, semen, pre-ejaculate, vaginal secretions, breast milk, saliva and tears;
  - » The most common ways to become infected are via unprotected vaginal, anal and, less commonly, oral sex, sharing of needles or equipment to inject drugs into veins, sharing of sex toys and the use of unsterilized needles for tattooing, skin piercing, or acupuncture. The risk of transmission through sharing of personal items, such as toothbrushes or razors, is low;
  - » Everyday casual physical contact with a person with HIV does not spread infection;
  - » Needle-stick injuries in health care settings can transmit the virus. In Canada blood and blood by-products are carefully screened for HIV. Only sterile needles are used for blood donations, making the risk of infection very, very low.
- Diagnosis:
  - » An HIV blood test for antibodies to the virus is used for diagnosis;
  - » If the test is negative, it should be repeated three months later, as it takes the body about three months to form the antibodies once infected. This can be done via a family doctor or STI/Public Health clinic;
  - » Testing can be anonymous if desired, but a positive test must be reported to Public Health, and partners located and tested. Partners should be protected from infection if they test negative.
- Treatment:
  - » There is no cure;
  - » New medications can prolong life and increase quality of life for persons infected with HIV;
  - » Treatment is complicated by the short- and long-term side effects of these drugs;
  - » There are also new strains of the virus causing resistance problems and treatment failures.

- Prevention:
  - » Prevention is key against this deadly disease;
  - » Having another STI increases your risk of becoming infected or transmitting the virus, so prevention against all STIs is best;
  - » High-risk groups include men who have sex with men, people with multiple partners, intravenous drug users, street-involved youth, sex-trade workers and their contacts;
  - » Only have sex with a partner willing to use condoms;
  - » Use latex condoms for all types of sex;
  - » Have only one partner who is sexually active only with you;
  - » Consider abstaining from or postponing intercourse. Caressing and touching are less risky;
  - » Have both you and your partner tested before starting a sexual relationship;
  - » Discuss STIs and HIV with your partner;
  - » Never share needles or injection equipment;
  - » Ensure body piercing or acupuncture equipment being used on you is sterile;
  - » If you have engaged in risky behaviour, get tested.
- Impact on Pregnancy:
  - » It is important to be tested in pregnancy. Some provinces are using universal screening of pregnant women since treatment with new medications can decrease the risk of transmission to the baby;
  - » The infection can be transmitted from an HIV-infected mother to her baby at birth or through breast milk.

Syphilis

- This sexually transmitted infection is caused by the spirochete treponema pallidum.
- Having previously been quite rare, syphilis began to increase in incidence again about five years ago. By 2002, Canada had four times the number of cases than it had in 1997.[87] It continues to increase in both male and females. Our national rate was 0.4 to 0.6 cases per 100,000 people in 1994, but was projected to be 0.9 cases per 100,000 in 2001.[88] The last five years

---

87 Health Canada, It's Your Health. Retrieved from www.hc-sc.gc.ca/english/iyh/index.html, January 10, 2005.
88 Public Health Association of Canada, STD Epi Update, Infectious Syphilis in Canada. Retrieved from www.phac-aspc.gc.ca/publicat/epiu-aepi/std-mts/infsyph_e.html, January 10, 2005.

have shown the largest increase in males aged 20 to 24, but incidence has also increased in males of all ages. There are regional differences in incidence: higher numbers are found in Vancouver among the sex-trade workers; among heterosexuals in the Yukon Territory; and in men having sex with men in Calgary, Vancouver, Montreal and Ottawa.[89] The World Health Association reported that syphilis is on the rise globally, with 12.2 million new cases in 1995.[90]

- Without treatment, the disease progresses through a series of five stages: primary, secondary, early latent, latent and tertiary.
- People remain infectious throughout the first three stages, which usually last about a year. When the infection becomes latent, it may progress to tertiary. The infection then damages brain tissue, blood vessels, heart and bones, and eventually leads to death.
- Symptoms:
  - » There may be no symptoms, thus making the infection hard to diagnose;
  - » If there are symptoms in the primary stage, they may be painless sores or ulcers at the site of entry, i.e., the genital area, throat or anus. This occurs within two to eight weeks of infection;
  - » The secondary stage symptoms are patchy hair loss, rash on the palms of the hands and soles of the feet or elsewhere, fever, sore glands, and muscle and joint pains.
- Transmission:
  - » This infection is spread through having oral, genital or anal sex with an infected person;
  - » Less commonly, the infection can be spread by intravenous drug use or by contact with broken skin somewhere on the body;
  - » The risk of contracting HIV is increased for people with syphilis. The genital ulcers of the primary stage cause a three to five times increase in the chance of becoming infected with HIV, if exposed. Those who are HIV positive and contract syphilis are at increased risk of transmitting the virus and are harder to treat.
- Diagnosis:
  - » The infection is diagnosed through a simple blood test. Follow-up testing is required after treatment. Partners must be notified and treated; this is a disease that is automatically reported to Public Health by the lab.

---

89   See preceding footnote.
90   Hook & Peeling, 2004.

- Treatment:
  - » Penicillin or other antibiotics easily cure syphilis;
  - » It is important to test for, diagnose and treat the infection early before it progresses and causes permanent damage.
- Prevention:
  - » Use condoms;
  - » Limit the number of sexual partners you have; talk to your partner about risk. Be tested;
  - » High-risk categories include people with more than one sexual partner, including men who have sex with men, heterosexuals, intravenous drug users and their partners, sex-trade workers and their clients and partners, people whose partners have syphilis, and people with other STIs.
- Impact on Pregnancy:
  - » Newborns can become infected at delivery; syphilis infection can cause birth defects or death in newborns;
  - » Women are now routinely screened during pregnancy with a blood test.

Hepatitis B

- Hepatitis B is an infection of the liver caused by a virus.
- It occurs throughout the world; in North America it affects mainly young adults, while in Africa and Asia it also affects infants and young children.
- There are estimated to be 350 million people worldwide with chronic persistent hepatitis B infection. Eleven million people die each year of this infection.[91]
- This infection is easier to get than HIV; it is 100 times more infective. Incidence in Canada in 1999 was 4.2 cases per 100,000.[92]
- Hepatitis B infects males more than females in a 2:1 ratio.
- After infecting an individual, the virus may go away on its own or it may persist.
- Ninety percent of adults will clear the virus from their system after an acute infection. There are many asymptomatic infections.
- Ten percent of people are carriers and can continue to carry the virus and remain infectious without knowing it.
- Fifteen to 40 percent of carriers develop continuous liver disease or cirrhosis; five to 10 percent of carriers will go on to develop liver cancer.

---

91   Public Health Agency of Canada, Bloodborne Pathogens Section, Hepatitis B Fact Sheet. Retrieved from www.phac-aspc.gc.ca/hcai-iamss/bbp-pts/hepatitis/hep_b_e.html, January 10, 2005.
92   See preceding footnote.

- The other 70 percent of carriers develop chronic persistent hepatitis B infection that is asymptomatic.
- Symptoms:
  - » The infection varies in severity; there can be no symptoms, mild to moderate symptoms, or severe illness;
  - » Poor appetite, nausea, vomiting, headache, general feeling of being unwell and sometimes jaundice can occur. Symptoms occur from six weeks to six months after exposure.
- Transmission:
  - » The infection is contracted through infected body fluids: blood, semen or vaginal fluid, or at birth. Therefore, the virus can be spread via sexual activity, blood exposure to infected fluids via needle-stick injuries, sharing of needles for IV drug use, sharing razors or toothbrushes, and human bites.
- Diagnosis:
  - » The infection is diagnosed through blood tests. If you are at risk, ask to be screened.
- Treatment:
  - » Treatment is given to relieve symptoms but there is no cure. Sometimes IV fluids and hospitalization are necessary for acute infections.
- Prevention:
  - » The good news is that Hepatitis B is the only STI preventable with immunization. In Ontario, Grade 7 students are routinely immunized through public health. Most provinces have incorporated this vaccine into their immunization schedule. The vaccine is given in two or three doses;
  - » Get immunized if you have not already done so;
  - » This vaccine is available free at STI clinics to those at high risk. Check your local phone book;
  - » High-risk persons include intravenous drug users and people having unprotected sex, especially with more than one partner. Use condoms; do not share needles, syringes, or equipment for body piercing, tattooing or hair removal. Do not share razors or toothbrushes.
- Impact on Pregnancy:
  - » Babies exposed at birth can be immunized at birth to prevent infection.

Crabs

- Pediculoses pubis are parasites that live in pubic hair. They feed on human blood.
- They cause a generalized itch and sometimes a rash.
- They are transmitted through skin-to-skin contact with an infected person. The lice can jump from pubic hair to pubic hair the way head lice do on the head. Head lice are a different type of lice from pubic lice.
- They can also be picked up from infested bedding and clothing.
- Treatment is available in the form of an over-the-counter liquid. This will kill any live lice but will not harm any eggs that may have been laid.
- A fine-tooth comb is used to remove the nits or eggs of the adult louse. The nits are not killed by the medicated lotion and will hatch five to 10 days later if they are not removed. If the eggs are left in place and hatch, the infestation will start all over again.
- Clothing, bedding and towels should be washed in hot water.

Bacterial Vaginosis

- This is a common, mild imbalance of the bacteria normally found in the vagina.
- It is often asymptomatic and need not be treated.
- Symptoms include change in vaginal discharge that may become grey and have a different, fishy smell. This can be tested for with a vaginal culture.
- Treatment for those who are symptomatic involves an intravaginal antibiotic gel or antibiotic by mouth.
- This infection is not usually spread between sexual partners and partners do not need treatment.

Urinary tract infections

- Vaginal intercourse predisposes women to bladder infections known as Urinary Tract Infections (UTIs).
- Symptoms:
  » A burning sensation when urinating;
  » Urinating more frequently than usual;
  » Back pain;
  » Fever;
  » Incontinence, which is the inability to control urination.
- If you experience any of the above symptoms, ask for a urine test at Health Services. UTIs are treated with antibiotics.

- There is some suggestion that drinking cranberry juice relieves symptoms, and may act as a preventative measure.
- You can lessen the likelihood of UTIs by urinating immediately after vaginal intercourse.

Emergency contraception
- The "Morning After Pill" can be used up to 72 hours after unprotected sex or contraceptive failure to prevent a pregnancy. It works by interfering with ovulation and preventing fertilization. It is more effective if taken sooner than 72 hours.
- All provinces now have it available "behind the counter" under the brand name "Plan B." No prescription is necessary. Ask to speak with the pharmacist who will likely discuss birth control and STIs with you before dispensing it.
- It decreases the risk of pregnancy by 75 percent.
- It may cause side effects, including nausea and vomiting, vaginal bleeding, headache, dizziness, breast tenderness, and fatigue.
- Gravol is sometimes given with one type of emergency contraceptive to decrease nausea.
- Common situations for its use include missing a birth control pill, a broken condom, a slipped diaphragm, or unplanned sex.
- It does not prevent STIs.

Condoms
- Initially condoms were developed as a barrier birth control method.
- Condoms provide birth control by preventing sperm from reaching the egg. If used properly, they are 97 percent effective. This can decrease to 90 percent if they are used incorrectly. It is important to read the instructions and put the condom on properly. Spermicides may increase the contraceptive effect when used with condoms, but offer no increased protection from STIs. If irritation occurs due to the chemical in spermicide, the risk of HIV transmission may actually increase.
- Now, with the increasing prevalence of STIs, the consistent use of condoms is a very important way to prevent becoming infected with or spreading these infections.
- The condom provides a barrier to keep the infected body fluids from passing the infection from one person to another.

- Latex or polyurethane condoms prevent STIs. Those made of natural sheep membranes do not.
- Condoms can be used to prevent STIs in vaginal, oral and anal sex, which is the riskiest form of sexual activity. A male or female condom can be cut lengthwise to use like a dental dam to fit over the female genitalia and anus during oral or anal sex. Refer to these Web sites for more information on using condoms:

  www.iwannaknow.org

  www.phac-aspc.gc.ca/std-mts/condoms_e.html
- Condoms are readily available and often free on campus, at Planned Parenthood offices, health centres and community health centres.
- They are sold in drug stores, vending machines in some public washrooms, and even on-line. When purchasing condoms, check the expiry date and check to be sure that the type you are considering protects against STIs.
- The type and fit are personal: a condom that is too big can slip off, and a condom that is too small can break.
- Condoms should be stored at room temperature and not subjected to heat, so don't carry them in your back pocket. If lubricant is used, it should be water-based only. Oil products such as Vaseline, baby oil and hand cream weaken latex condoms.
- Should a condom break during sexual activity, consider emergency contraception as outlined on page 232. See a doctor for STI screening and treatment if necessary.
- Convince your partner of the benefits of safer sex with condoms. Say no if the person is unwilling.

References

American Social Health Association, Facts and Answers about STDs. Retrieved from http://www.ashastd.org/stdfaqs/index.html, January 10, 2005.

Health Canada, It's Your Health. Retrieved from www.hc-sc.gc.ca/english/iyh/index.html, January 10, 2005.

Hook, III, E. W., and Peeling, R. W., 2004, Syphilis Control – A Continuing Challenge, *The New England Journal of Medicine*, Volume 351, 2, pages 122-124.

Patrick, D., Wong, T., Jordan, R., 2000, Sexually Transmitted Infections In Canada; Recent Resurgence Threatens National Goals. *The Canadian Journal of Human Sexuality*, Vol. 9 (3).

Public Health Agency of Canada, Bloodborne Pathogens Section, Hepatitis B Fact Sheet. Retrieved from www.phac-aspc.gc.ca/hcai-iamss/bbp-pts/hepatitis/hep_b_e.html, January 10, 2005.

Public Health Agency of Canada, Centre for Infectious Diseases Prevention and Control, Sexual Health and Sexually Transmitted Infections Section. Reported cases and rates of notifiable sexually transmitted infections from January 1 to March 31, 2004. Retrieved from http://www.phac-aspc.gc.ca/std-mts/stdcases-casmts/index.html, January 10, 2005.

Public Health Association of Canada, Sexual Health and STIs, Condoms. Retrieved from www.phac-aspc.gc.ca/std-mts/condoms_e.html, January 10, 2005.

Public Health Association of Canada, STD Epi Update, Infectious Syphilis in Canada. Retrieved from www.phac-aspc.gc.ca/publicat/epiu-aepi/std-mts/infsyph_e.html, January 10, 2005.

Public Health Agency of Canada, Home: Publications: Epi Update 2004, Chapter 1. HIV/AIDS Epi Update – May 2004. Retrieved from http://www.phac-aspc.gc.ca/publicat/epiu-aepi/epi_update_may_04/1_e.html, January 10, 2005.

Public Health Agency of Canada, Home: Publications: Epi Update 2004, Chapter 2 HIV/AIDS Epi Update – May 2004. Retrieved from http://www.phac-aspc.gc.ca/publicat/epiu-aepi/epi_update_may_04/2_e.html, January 10, 2005.

Public Health Agency of Canada, Home; Publications: Epi Update 2004, Chapter 5 HIV/AIDS Epi Update – May 2004. Retrieved from http://www.phac-aspc.gc.ca/publicat/epiu-aepi/epi_update_may_04/5_e.html, January 10, 2005.

Public Health Agency of Canada, Home: Publications: Epi Update 2004, Chapter 11 HIV/AIDS Epi Update – May 2004. Retrieved from http://www.phac-aspc.gc.ca/publicat/epiu-aepi/epi_update_may_04/11_e.html, January 10, 2005.

Additional sources used indirectly in the preparation of Appendix 4

American Social Health Association, Answers to your questions about teen sexual health. Retrieved from www.iwannaknow.org/, January 10, 2005.

American Social Health Association, Prevention, Condoms. Retrieved from www.iwannaknow.org/prevention/condoms.html#5, January 10, 2005.

Bryson, S.C.P., 1999, Treatment for genital warts in women. *Patient Care Canada*, Vol. 10, No. 2.

Canadian Centre for Occupational Health and Safety, Biological Hazards, Diseases, Disorders and Injuries, Hepatitis B. Retrieved from www.ccohs.ca/oshanswers/diseases/hepatitis_b.html, January 10, 2005.

Government of Canada, Youth Health. Retrieved from http://chp-
pcs.gc.ca/CHP/index_e.jsp/pageid/4005/odp/Top/Health/Youth/Sexuality/Sexually_
Transmitted_Infections/Chlamydia, January 10, 2005.

Howard, M., Sellars, J., Jung, D., Robinson, N., Fearon, M., Kaczorowski, J.,
Chernesky, M., 2003, Regional Distribution of Antibodies to Herpes Simplex
Virus Type 1 (HSV-1) and HSV-2 in Men and Women in Ontario, Canada. *Journal
of Clinical Microbiology*, Vol. 41 (1) p. 84-89.

Public Health Agency of Canada, STD Epi Update, May 2002. Retrieved from
www.phac-aspc.gc.ca/publicat/epiu-aepi/std-mts/condom_e.html, January 10,
2005.

Public Health Agency of Canada, What you need to know about sexually
transmitted infections. Retrieved from http://www.phac-aspc.gc.ca/publicat/std-
mts/sti_g.html, January 10, 2005.

Public Health Association of Canada, Health Info for everybody. Retrieved from
www.canadian-health-network.ca, January 10, 2005.

Telner, D., 2001, STDs in Primary Care. *Patient Care Canada*, Vol.12, No. 1.

Tetrault, I. and Boivin, G., 2000, Recent Advances in the Management of Genital
Herpes. *Canadian Family Physician*, Vol. 46.

The College of Family Physicians of Canada, STIs – Common STIs and tips on
prevention. Retrieved from
www.cfpc.ca/English/cfpc/programs/patient%20education/sti/default.asp?s=1,
January 10, 2005.

Steinberg, W.F., 2004, STDs in Reproductive-Age Women: The Growing Epidemic.
Patient Care Canada, Vol. 15, No. 12.

Vezina, C. and Steben, M., 2001, Psychosocial Impact of Human Papilloma Virus,
The Canadian Journal of CME, June, 2001.

Would you like to order copies of
University Matters
or
University Matters Student Planner
for your friends or family?

To order, visit our Web site at
www.universitymatters.ca
or call **1-800-287-8610**.

To arrange bulk orders or inquire
about fundraising initiatives,
e-mail us at
bulkorders@universitymatters.ca